10 99

D0283296

PORCUPINE
PEOPLE

241.4 E99P c.1
Ezell, Lee.
Porcupine people : learning
to love the unlovable /

PROPERTY OF
HIGH POINT PUBLIC LIBRARY
HIGH POINT, NORTH CAROLINA

PROPERTY OF
HIGH POINT PUBLIC LIBRARY
HIGH POINT, NORTH CAROLINA

Porcupine People

LEARNING TO LOVE
THE UNLOVABLE

LEE EZELL

SERVANT PUBLICATIONS
ANN ARBOR, MICHIGAN

PROPERTY OF
HIGH POINT PUBLIC LIBRARY
HIGH POINT, NORTH CAROLINA

© 1998 by Lee Ezell
All rights reserved.

Vine Books is an imprint of Servant Publications especially designed to serve evangelical Christians.

Unless otherwise noted, the Scripture used is from the *New King James Version* (NKJV), © 1979, 1980, 1982, 1990, Thomas Nelson Inc., Publishers; *The Message: The New Testament in Contemporary Language* by Eugene H. Peterson, ©1993, used by permission of NavPress Publishing Group; the *New American Standard Bible* (NASB), © 1960, 1962, 1963, 1968, 1971, 1972, 1973, 1975, 1977, The Lockman Foundation. Verses marked NIV are from the *New International Version*.

Lyric excerpts of "Do You Love Me," by Sheldon Harnick and Jerry Bock, © 1964 by Alley Music Corp. and Trio Music Company, Inc. Copyright renewed in 1992 and reassigned to Mayerling Productions, Ltd., and Jerry Bock Enterprises for the United States, and to Alley Music Corp., Trio Music Company, and Jerry Bock Enterprises for all other territories. Reprinted by permission. All rights reserved.

In some cases, names and identifying characteristics have been changed to protect the privacy of the individuals whose stories are told in this book.

Included in this book are quotes and quips for which every effort was made to cite the original source. The publisher would be happy to correct any omissions in future reprints, if notified in writing by the copyright holder.

Published by Servant Publications
P.O. Box 8617
Ann Arbor, Michigan 48107

Cover design: Hile Illustration and Design

98 99 00 10 9 8 7 6 5 4 3 2 1

Printed in the United States of America
ISBN 1-56955-105-7

LIBRARY OF CONGRESS CATALOGING-IN-PUBLICATION DATA

Ezell, Lee.
    Porcupine people : learning to love the unloveable / Lee Ezell.
        p.   cm.
    Includes bibliographical references (p.   ).
    ISBN 1-56955-105-7 (alk. paper)
    1. Love—Religious aspects—Christianity.   2. Interpersonal relations—Religious aspects—Christianity.   I. Title.
BV4639.E94   1998
241'.4—dc21   98-28979   CIP

Dedication

To Edna Ezell, Nana, a mother-in-law I can't make any jokes about. Thank you for being a living example of unconditional love for porcupine people.

Contents

Foreword

Lee Ezell has a wonderful gift for helping us to look at our shortcomings with honesty and humor, all the while calling us to reach out for God's best for our lives. She does it again in *Porcupine People*. I always enjoy and am challenged by what Lee has to share but I feel that this book is particularly significant because it addresses a command that Jesus gave to us at the end of his ministry. As he was telling his disciples that he would not be with them much longer, he then said, "A new commandment I give you: love one another. As I have loved you so you must love one another." And then he went on to say that our love for each other would actually be our ID badge showing that we belong to him. "By this will all men know that you are my disciples, if you love one another" (Jn 13:34, NIV).

I believe that within that command lies the secret to accomplishing the Great Commission. And it's a choice—loving is a choice! In *Porcupine People*, Lee Ezell helps us journey down the road of unconditional love—learning to love the unlovely, even as Jesus loved us. I think of the old hymn, He looked beyond my fault and saw my need.

God is amassing an army today. He's looking for recruits who are willing to do more than just talk about loving one another. He's looking for recruits who are willing to get up out of their pews and embrace each other and a hurting, searching world with his unconditional love. In this day and age as the eye of God searches to and fro across the land saying, "Who shall I send?" let us respond resoundingly as Isaiah did, "Here am I. Send me!" (Is 6:8).

Terry Meeuwsen
Cohost, "The 700 Club"

Acknowledgments

This book is affectionately written out of my own need to better love the porcupine people in my life. The principles reflected here have been hammered out in a personal forge of relationships and tested by the scores of folks who attend my seminars. They are offered in the hope of drawing both your heart and your head to the Lord of love who challenged us:

> A new commandment I give to you, that you love one another; as I have loved you.
>
> JOHN 13:34

Introduction

Peggy had an eerie feeling as she turned the key in the front door—something wasn't right. As she glanced inside, she had that familiar sinking feeling in her stomach. "No, Ronnie, no, not again!" she cried. Yes, her prodigal son, Ron, had broken into the house, once more turning to burglary in a desperate effort to support his drug habit. The stereo was gone, the TV cabinet was empty, and Peggy could only guess what else was missing as she rushed upstairs. Her heart sank further as she saw her bedroom was a mess and her jewelry drawer emptied. Peggy collapsed into a heap, sobbing and swearing to herself that she would never again trust Ron. Facts were facts: she couldn't afford to love her son anymore.

Can Peggy continue to love her son without denying the reality of his character?

* * *

"There's no sparkle anymore. It's just routine boredom," Casey whispered to herself as she pulled into her driveway. She felt nothing for Gary like the spark of excitement she felt listening to Pastor Tim at Bible study. "Now *there's* a godly man, who knows how to treat a woman," she smiled. A slight flush of embarrassment warmed her, as she realized how drawn she was to another man. Wasn't that just further evidence that she and Gary had lost touch? Staring out the windshield after turning off the motor, Casey knew Gary would be wondering why she was late coming home. She told herself it was good that she was finally coming out of her denial. Wasn't it about time she faced the fact she didn't love her husband anymore? If she had ever loved him, they had by now fallen out of love. Gary no longer met her needs. She promised herself that tonight they would talk turkey.

Can Casey find her way back to that lovin' feelin' for her husband?

* * *

Ray watched the cars filling the church parking lot on Sunday morning. *What fools!* he thought. *They all file in, hear some religious platitudes and a few Bible verses, and for what? I was a sincere believer, too, but a lot of good it did me! God was apparently busy elsewhere when I needed him most. If there is a loving God, how could he let my best friend betray me?*

Ray's friend Carl had been his best man at his wedding, and they had gone to the same church for years. But when they decided to go into business together, it lasted for only a few months. Carl convinced Ray to sign some papers that virtually put the profits into his own (Carl's) pocket. When Ray realized what had happened, Carl justified what he'd done and twisted Ray's anger back against him saying, "See, you're not a spiritual man. I can't partner with you." He'd taken the money and started a business of his own.

Can Ray ever again be a friend to Carl?

* * *

Hanging up the phone, Laurie couldn't believe she was actually back in the dating scene, though she knew it was inevitable. After two and a half years of being single, both she (and her kids) would be meeting an assortment of suitors. But immediately after she accepted the invitation to dinner, Laurie began asking herself the same old questions she'd pondered so many times: *How in the world can I tell if a man is sincere? (He could even be married, and I wouldn't know.) Are there men who understand fidelity? (The ones I've known think monogamy is a type of wood.)* After the unfaithfulness of her ex, Laurie was tempted to conclude she'd be better off resigning herself to being single forever.

Can Laurie risk loving again after bitter disappointment?

Are You Willing to Take a Risk?

Do you know any of these people? Perhaps you identify with Peggy, Casey, Ray or Laurie. If you are dealing with a porcupine person, someone who has hurt you in the past with toxic responses or behavior, this book is for you. Porcupine people are not just the homeless, the rude, the outcasts of society and family. Sometimes porcupine people wear designer suits, drive nice cars and occupy prestigious positions in the community. They are our friends and neighbors, spouses, children, parents, brothers and sisters in the Lord. Their emotional quills rise when threatened with confrontation, accountability and even love. Reaching out to them can hurt you. The easy way out is to relegate porcupine people to your "Do Not Touch" social category.

But you and I have a choice. Jesus did not say, "This is my *suggestion,* that you love one another." He used the word *commandment* (Jn 15:10-12). If we are going to walk in the light of Christ, we can't just give up on someone because that person is hard to love.

There is something you and I can do to trigger God's flow of love for the difficult people in our lives. The truths in the following chapters are intended to empower you to trust again in spite of disillusioning experiences you may have faced. Like buried treasure, hidden far below the hardened surface, you can unearth a flow of compassion by using the tools God has provided.

But wouldn't it be foolish to risk being hurt again? If you are asking this question, your heart is right, but you may just lack the tools and know-how to love others as God has loved you. Here is hope from a writer who once had reason to give up on healthy relationships. There were an increasing number of porcupine people in my life that would have been easier for me to avoid and reject. Then I realized the world is full of people who are lost because they have not been loved. I began to look for ways to bring back that lovin' feelin' for the porcupine people in my life.

Are you wondering if Peggy, Casey, Ray or Laurie will be able to recover trust and love and to enjoy full, true and joy-filled lives again? Will you? I pray what I have learned will encourage you to fulfill Jesus' commandment and to risk loving porcupine people again.

Part I

Learning the Lessons of Love

ONE

The Fruit of Love

Why is it we struggle to get along with certain people? Some make a career of disagreeing with our favorite opinions. Others seem to spend years determining what kind of behavior annoys us most and then act out their unique version of it the minute we enter their peripheral vision. Still others have hurt us—really hurt us—and we've never quite forgotten or forgiven the wound. We find it hard to live with the fact they choose to injure us, sometimes again and again. I hope you'll catch the vision of how to love those who are as hard to embrace as porcupines, and how to avoid getting hurt by these prickly people.

More often than not, the people who cause us the most stress are those we care about a great deal. In fact, the folks who get on our nerves most are often those by whom we wish to be loved most. After all, we love them, or at least we used to. I suggest that as you read this book, you focus on the one difficult, unlovable person who troubles you most. You've most likely been stuck by his or her abrasive porcupine quills in more than one conversation or situation. Who qualifies? All those who have their quills out, radiating the message "Do not touch me!" It could be ...

- your mother-in-law
- your daughter's boyfriend
- an ex-girlfriend
- that obnoxious guy (or gal) in the church choir
- your grandma
- an argumentative left-wing liberal uncle
- a pro-choice feminist sister.

These people look and smell nice, but they respond unkindly when threatened. This is part of their self-protection system. Like their counterparts in the animal kingdom, the quills of porcupine people don't shoot out; you can only be hurt by reaching out to touch one of them. And if you get close, everything within you says, *Beware!* The easy way out is to justify giving up on these people by remembering your past scars. *Ouch!* But if you and I are going to walk in the light with Christ, then we must give it another try.

I am painfully aware that, from time to time, we make wholehearted efforts to genuinely care for porcupine people. But every time we reach out, we get stuck by a hurtful remark, thoughtless behavior or some disappointing reaction that reminds us—too late—we promised never to put ourselves in that position again. It is a perfectly natural response to recoil and decide not to risk that. After all, we're not fools, are we? They may look good, these prickly porcupine people, yet when their toxic responses hit us, it doesn't feel good. But are we free to simply walk away from difficult or painful relationships?

Speaking on this subject always causes me to whisper a prayer for wisdom: "Open our eyes, Lord. We may not see things as clearly as we should." The person with whom you are most upset may be someone you cannot escape. It may be an employer. A neighbor. A difficult relative. Or the course of your life may have changed suddenly, disrupting every relationship and leaving you filled with doubt and despair. You may even be having a hard time loving God.

We've All Been Hurt

Hurt, disappointment and lost love are universal human experiences. Every person is touched by one of these at some point in his or her life. I am a ripe candidate for writing a book on learning to love porcupine people again because I've loved ... and been hurt. Born into an abusive home, I was raised by alcoholic parents in Philadelphia's inner city. I keenly understood what is meant by the modern term "dysfunctional family." By contemporary standards I may be justified in an unloving attitude because I could describe my formative years in psychobabble something like this:

"I had inadequate role models in my dysfunctional family of origin. When my shame-based behavior became codependent, my inner child suffered a nurturing deficiency. Eventually she died from malnutrition!"

In fact, my family of origin did fail me, and early on I lost a sense of belonging and worth. Looking back, I guess I thought I was from the shallow end of the gene pool. My two older sisters married young in order to leave home; at seventeen, I jumped ship myself. I came to Christ at a Billy Graham crusade. Not too many months later, I was raped. That horrifying experience virtually convinced me that I could never trust a man—or God, for that matter—ever again. That wasn't the end of it, either. Soon I realized the rape had left me pregnant. Without family support or any way to care for a child, I gave up my baby girl for adoption. She was the only child to whom I would ever give birth.

Not surprisingly, whatever fragile self-love I'd possessed quickly slipped away at this point. After all, I was a loser, a gal who apparently had a knack for being in the wrong place at the wrong time. I seemed to attract losers like a white silk blouse attracts spots. My father had always told me my birth was a mistake, and that was reinforced by my experiences. Of course, I didn't confirm the fact that I was a loser by telling anyone about the rape. At the time, I fully expected to carry this secret to my grave. But this experience gave me an early start in piling up life's regrets. The porcupine people in my life included many individuals besides the man who raped me. At times, it included myself, too.

After giving up my baby, I assumed love and marriage would be one phase of life that I could expect to live without. I didn't believe I was lovable. How could I? I didn't even like myself, so the thought of feeling warm and fuzzy toward a husband ... well, that seemed like an impossible dream. Neither was my track record for good decision making all that hot. Again and again I questioned myself: Had I made the right choice in relinquishing my child? Had God guided me in that decision? As my sense of isolation and struggle increased, I began to long for more of the Lord. Gradually, I began to seek him, to try to find out what his character was like, to see if he could honestly be counted on to keep that which I had committed unto him (see 2 Tm 1:12). I was learning, as an old hymn encouraged, to seek the Lord "beyond the sacred page."

I hadn't been brought up in a church. I didn't speak the jargon. I didn't understand the Christian culture. I was an outsider when I began attending services. When I suggested to my Baptist singles group that we have a square dance or a Monte Carlo night to raise money for the budget, they were horrified, and I was humiliated by their reaction. In numerous churches and outreach ministries between the birth of my child and my marriage ten years later, I was confronted with disappointing Christian leadership. Sometimes a preacher fell prey to one of the three biggies: sex, power or money. I watched church boards split and crumble. I saw funds misused as the fund thermometer rose. Self-righteous individuals caused me to feel betrayed, and at times forsaken, by God's people. When I met good people, I often dealt with the gnawing question, "Where were they when I needed them?" Little by little, as I campaigned for worthwhile causes, I became negative and cynical. But personal knowledge of God saved me from relying solely on the poor representation of Christ I saw in some churches.

What You See, You Get?

Comedian Flip Wilson used to say, "What you see, honey, is what you get!" I propose a question for your consideration: Is beauty—or goodness, grace or generosity—in the eye of the beholder? Why do some people see goodness where others see only evil? Why do some see graceful swans when others see gawky ducks?

I once heard a speaker relate the story of two boys who were discussing eyeglasses. "Wouldn't you hate to wear glasses?" one asked.

"No, not really," answered the other, "not if I could have the kind my grandma wears. My mother says she can always see when folks are tired or discouraged or sad. She sees when somebody is in need and she can always recognize when you have something on your mind that you need to talk over. Best of all, she is able to see something good in everybody!"

Some say love is blind. But if love makes us blind, marriage is a real eye-opener. Before I married my husband, Hal, he was my prince. Later, I feared I'd kissed him too much because he seemed to have reverted back into a frog. My early dating impressions were of a thrifty, sensitive man of few words. I guess you could say he was the strong, silent type. I was enchanted.

Not long after we were married, however, I started to gain a somewhat different perspective of Hal's traits. I remember looking at his picture in my wallet and sighing, "I will always treasure the false image I had of you...."

Hal wasn't thrifty; he was a miser.

Hal wasn't sensitive, either; pushover was closer to the truth.

As for the strong, silent type? Hal was stubborn; he refused to communicate. When he told me I had "verbal diarrhea," I

responded that it was just as well—he was completely consti-
pated in that area.

Romance was fast fading, at least in my eyes. I was beginning
to think, *I don't love him. I don't even like him anymore. I married him for all the wrong reasons.*

The word *love* has been defined, dissected, deciphered and
decoded by greater experts than I. But there are a couple of
points worth clarifying right here, right now: love is far more
than an emotion. It is a decision. It is a lifelong mission.

> ove is an UNCONDITIONAL commitment
> to an IMPERFECT person.

What Is This Thing Called Love?

We will never receive the *gift* of love. In fact, if you can find
someone who can lay hands on you and impart this gift,
please call me! The Bible says love is a *fruit,* not a gift. When
we read listings of the New Testament gifts of the Spirit (see
Rom 12 and 1 Cor 12), we find that love is not listed among
them. But when we review the fruit of the Spirit, it is the first
characteristic listed.

But the fruit of the Spirit is: love, joy, peace, patience, kindness, goodness, faithfulness, gentleness and self-control.

GALATIANS 5:22-23 NIV

As a fruit, love has to grow, and that requires effort, nurturing and wise tending of the orchard. If we can prune away whatever stands in the way of love and begin to cultivate the attitudes that foster love, love will take root and blossom inside us. We must weed out roots of bitterness, jealousy, unforgiveness, disappointment and other negative emotions to prepare the soil. Love is much more than an emotion, a sensation, affection or feeling. We promise ourselves, "Well, when I genuinely feel love for my teenage son, I'll show it." (If that's your attitude, by the way, pack in for the winter; you may be waiting until he's twenty-five!) Love is a way of acting, not a feeling on which we base our actions. Often we have to act before we feel. I believe it was Brother Lawrence who wrote,

> All things are possible to those who believe, but all things are easier to those who believe and LOVE!

All the other fruits of the Spirit follow love and, in fact, stem from love. None of us automatically or magically received these virtues the moment we received God's gift of life in Jesus Christ. Because they are fruits, not gifts, they must be desired, planted, cultivated and pruned. We may even have a little fertilizer thrown on us now and then—that promotes growth too, you know!

As we continue the process of learning to love again—or learning to love in the first place—we will consider many kinds of love, and, of course, we will include the love we have, or once had, or think we've lost, for our spouses. But no matter whom we're talking about, under what conditions or in what stage of life:

> ## Love is seeing God's beauty where others do not.

Things are always changing. Or is it our *attitudes* that are always changing? We take a job that seems perfect but soon find ourselves in the midst of office politics and backbiting. We buy what we think is our dream car, but soon its windows don't work, it makes a weird noise in third gear and gets dirty too quickly. We are sure the answer to our church's problem is a new building, then we find ourselves launching full speed into fund-raising sermons, fund-raising envelopes and fund-raising picnics that create more questions than answers.

Did the job, the car or the church change? Perhaps a little. But it's likely our attitude changed more because our focus changed. In my marriage, Hal hadn't done an overnight Dr. Jekyll–Mr. Hyde transformation. In truth, nothing about Hal had changed. But time, familiarity and circumstances had changed my point of view. I wasn't seeing the beauty any-more—only the beast. The truth is that both beauty and beast are present in each one of us, as the following sketch illustrates:

Do you see the lovely young princess?

Or do you see the ugly old witch?

What you see is what you get! Once you see both characters, you can choose the one on which you want to focus. Maybe we should consider this factor in learning to see porcupine people in a positive light once again.

Beauty Is in the Eye

Finding myself in emotionally dark places, I've come to see a sort of creeping cynicism has taken over my way of looking at things. Where I once enjoyed a happy-go-lucky, live-and-let-live attitude, I'd entertain doubts. I was seeing porcupine people everywhere. I'd watch Christian TV and sneer at the hosts: *Are they for real?* I'd go to church, wondering how many hypocrites were actually there. I'd see a middle-aged man holding the hand of a younger woman and think to myself, *He's probably not even supporting his ex-wife and children*. Reading these words of warning from the Lord Jesus, I realized what was happening:

> The lamp of your body is your eye. When your eye is sound, your whole body is full of light. But when your eye is evil, your whole body is full of darkness. So be very careful that your light never becomes darkness.
>
> LUKE 11:34-36 PHILLIPS

The Scriptures say that "God is light and in him is no darkness at all" (1 Jn 1:5). Christ said, "the pure in heart ... shall see God" (Mt 5:8). The purity of heart was draining out of me, as my eye was becoming pessimistic and disapproving.

Do You Have an Eye for Beauty?

Tim Hansel tells the story of two bedridden elderly gentlemen living in a convalescent hospital. They shared a room at the hospital, which was nestled into scenic countryside, but only one of them could see out the window. The patient farther from the window looked forward to that time each day when his roommate struggled up onto his elbows at the window and gave the daily report of what he could see. "Oh!" he'd exclaim, "today is a perfect spring day. There are two young girls walking their dogs—one girl is blond, one is brunette; one is walking a miniature poodle, one is walking a big dalmatian. There are a couple of boys leaning over the pond, sailing little homemade boats. And it looks like everyone is gearing up for the parade. The reviewing stands are being set up down the street. There's excitement in the air!"

As the weeks went by, the man who had lived for those moments, picturing them all day in his mind's eye, began to feel jealous. Why did his roommate have the view? Why couldn't the two of them be rotated? Jealousy soon became resentment, and that became hatred. In his bitterness, before long he didn't even want to hear the daily reports anymore.

It was during this time, in the middle of the night, that his friend by the window had a choking bout and was so stricken that he couldn't reach the call button for the nurse. The jealous man lay there pretending to be asleep—until the choking stopped. Early the next morning the nurse came in. She sadly announced, "Oh no! He's gone." He had choked to death.

The roommate restrained his joy, thinking that soon they would move his bed over to the window. He bothered the staff all morning until they relocated him. Immediately he lifted himself up to capture his first glimpse of beauty outside. To his amazement, all he could see was a brick wall. There was nothing to look at; there never had been. The beauty had only been "seen" through the imaginative and loving eyes of his friend.[1] This story raises several questions: some are about issues of jealousy and lack of gratitude, others about friendship and generosity. But the biggest question is about the reality of what we see. Is there such a thing as seeing with loving, imaginative eyes?

> Faith works by love.

Some churches hold a regular foot-washing service. Maybe we should propose an "eye-washing" service, too. As we consider the A-B-C steps to loving again in the following pages, let's prepare to take the beams out of our own eyes so we can see more clearly. As we open ourselves to the light of truth, our vision will be cleansed, and we will find ourselves walking in the light. What's more, we'll have fellowship with porcupine people!

Reflections

1. Who is the most obvious porcupine person in your life? List him or her, along with others, in order of prickliness.

2. Describe the two sides of your porcupine person (or persons). List their strengths and weaknesses.

3. Do you have difficulty loving yourself? Write out the reasons why. List your strengths and your weaknesses.

4. Is it hard for you to trust God? If so, take time to consider why. Write out your reasons. Ask God to give you new insights into trust.

5. Ask God to guide you as you continue to seek reconciliation with him, yourself, your spouse and family or other individuals who represent a challenge to you.

TWO

Learn to Love—Why Bother?

Julio was part of a Costa Rican teenage street gang that supported its criminal habits through an ongoing burglary ring. One day while removing prize possessions from a house, Julio was caught red-handed by some Christian homeowners. Once apprehended, he was terrified. He slumped in a chair, glared at the floor and assumed the police would arrive and haul him off to jail. *Not the first time in jail,* he reminded himself, *and probably not the last.*

But the Christian couple had a different idea about Julio's future. They decided to refer the case to a higher authority than local law enforcement. *Why not take a chance on the kid,* they thought, *and try to influence him for God?* As Julio sat in their home grimly awaiting his fate, they began talking to him about his behavior. Why was he stealing? What was it he needed? What had caused him to turn to crime? Had the couple justifiably confronted Julio, his porcupine quills would have risen and a major argument would have been launched.

After hearing his not-so-inspiring story, the couple gently explained their spiritual commitment. "We are believers in Jesus Christ," they told him. "Jesus loved us and died for us even

33

though we were sinners, even though we were always breaking God's laws. We want you to know that Jesus loves you, too. And so do we. We want to help you, not get you thrown in jail!"

The couple cared about Julio in spite of his obvious sin. They were visual aids, dramatically illustrating the undeserved favor of God. They not only talked about grace; they *became* grace to Julio. He was speechless. *What is wrong with these strange people?* he wondered. *Ten minutes ago, I broke into their house and started carrying away their treasures. Now they're trying to help me?*

Not long afterward, my friends Mike and Jenni Ramsey headed up a Youth With A Mission team in Costa Rica. When they arrived to conduct a street meeting in Julio's depressed area, they found him sitting patiently, waiting for instructions about how to receive Christ. He told them why he had come to the meeting—because of the Christian couple who had loved him. Julio needed little explanation of God's love since he had already seen it in action. That night he gladly gave his life to Christ, exclaiming after he prayed, "I feel so clean inside!"

Jesus has called us to be lovers of all people, everywhere—the good, the bad and the ugly. But that includes more than strangers like Julio who require dramatic acts of forgiveness, poverty-stricken tribespeople safely removed by a dozen time zones or acquaintances who have little impact on us. Our mandate to love includes the people close by, the troublemakers we have the most reason to resent, the transgressors we love to hate and the annoying folks we'd simply prefer to ignore.

Excuses, Excuses

I don't have to tell you that loving isn't easy. But we make loving even harder on ourselves. We have a quick answer prepared for every person we should learn to love, scripted to excuse us from our responsibility to take the necessary risks. We say,

- "But you see, trying to love my son after all his rejection and separation is too painful. Yes, I feel the loss, but it is easier to deal with it this way. To call him is to open a can of worms and expose old wounds. I'd have to be a masochist to try loving him again."

- "But you don't know how many times I've tried. The fact is, loving my mother never does any good. She'll never change. She continues to hurt me every chance I give her. Why should I be stupid enough to volunteer for that abuse again?"

- "No, I've struggled too long. It's over between my husband and me. We've both accepted that. Shutting him out of my life is much easier than trying to reason with him. The sad truth is that we don't love each other anymore; we're just staying together for the kids."

Can you imagine the excuses that Christian couple in Costa Rica could have given for turning Julio over to the authorities?

- "Now that he's been inside our house, he knows where everything is. He'll be back, and next time he'll bring his friends."

- "Kids like that are hard cases; there's no point trying to reach them with Christian ideas. They are bad to the core."

- "Oh, right. Sure! Of course he'll go along with our Christian witnessing because guys like that are natural con artists. Listen, you can't trust anybody, especially not people who are caught in the act of stealing you blind! Come off it!"

Our excuses make a lot of sense to us. They hold up pretty well when we say them out loud. But when we compare them with God's Word and the love of Jesus, our reasons for refusing to love don't sound as convincing as we'd like them to.

Here's the bottom line: if we are serious about walking with God and doing what pleases him, we've got to swallow our pride, squelch our mistrust and stifle our excuses. The benefits and advantages of choosing to love, learning to love and deciding to love again are worth the struggle it takes to get over our worst fears.

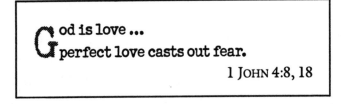

God is love ...
perfect love casts out fear.

1 JOHN 4:8, 18

So God expects us to love everybody? But then, some of his other ideas are a little far-fetched, too, aren't they? Lay down our lives for our friends and die to ourselves? That's just for saints, right?

Wrong! God's expectations for us are not as far-fetched as we'd like to think. But since obedience doesn't come easily, it might be helpful if we get a handle on why being a loving person is a good idea.

Love Is God's Commandment

Did you ever sing that upbeat chorus in church that goes, "This is my suggestion, that you love one another ..."? Oh, you haven't heard that one? Probably not! When he told us to love each other, Jesus was not putting an idea in the suggestion box for our consideration. It is only because of our hurts, fears and selfishness that we act as if love is a recommendation. The God of the universe never advised us to love. He commanded it. Maybe we should listen to our heavenly Father, who says, *Why love? Because I'm God and I said so!*

> If you keep my commandments you will abide in my love.... This is my commandment, that you love one another.
>
> JOHN 15:10, 12 NASB

We have been called to love, but the old adage is true: God's *callings* are God's *enablings.* I take courage in the fact that God will never command me to do something without giving me the power to do it! Once we make the commitment to obey, God begins to move. He strengthens our resolve. He empowers our ability. He changes our attitudes. The decision is ours; the ability to act is his. Our loving responses empowered by his Holy Spirit are the results of that decision.

Of course, there are excellent fringe benefits. For one thing, when we obey the Father's commandment to love, we become candidates for friendship with him. He and his Son, Jesus

Christ, will become real in our life when we dedicate ourselves to keeping the commandment by choosing to love.

> You are my friends, if you do what I command you.
>
> JOHN 15:14 NASB

> Whoever has my commands and obeys them, he is the one who loves me. He who loves me will be loved by my Father, and I too will love him and show myself to him.
>
> JOHN 14:21 NIV

There are many other good reasons to love, all of them beneficial to us in spirit, mind and body. Here are more of his wise parental reasons:

Love Fulfills All God's Laws

> Love does no harm to its neighbor. Therefore love is the fulfillment of the law.
>
> ROMANS 13:10 NIV

Look at it this way: if you develop the habit of deferring to love, you won't need to tediously study all the other commandments of God. Without realizing it, you will be fulfilling them.

When faced with God's requirements, folks defensively say, "Well, I keep the Ten Commandments." Really? Can you even name all ten? Can you imagine being able to obey all of God's

PROPERTY OF
HIGH POINT PUBLIC LIBRARY
HIGH POINT NORTH CAROLINA

laws, requirements and directives? Most of us can't get past the first one: "Love the Lord your God with all your heart, and with all your soul, and with all your mind" (Mt 22:37). Yet Jesus himself linked this impossible task to the second: "Love your neighbor as yourself" (Mt 22:39). Instead of racking your brain, imagine instead that you can have such love that you'll "have no other God" before him, because God is the source of all your loving. Imagine yourself being able to give real "honor" to your father and mother because you love. Or how could any of us kill, steal, bear false witness if we truly loved? Even our tendency to covet will begin to melt away when love is in charge.

There's more. The injunctions of Jesus in what we call the Beatitudes (see Mt 5) begin to come alive when we adopt a loving spirit. We gain a greater understanding of what "Blessed are the meek ..." means. We will become more "merciful." We will find ourselves in the role of "peacemaker." In short, God's law will be fulfilled in our love for others.

Love Is Our Distinguishing Mark

Let's be honest: does the world really recognize Christians as loving people? Sometimes I wonder when I see God's people reacting with venomous words of disagreement to those who oppose them. I grieve when I see believers so incensed about issues that people behind the issues fall victim to misnamed "righteous indignation."

I am frequently saddened by women and men who speak fluent "Christianese," yet who haven't got a clue about how to get along with people of diverse denominations, not to mention of other world religions. Love? Some Christians appear not to even like anyone but their own crowd of insiders. Baptists attend Baptist conventions, charismatics only charismatic ones. Conservatives wouldn't be caught dead at a Save the Earth rally. But God divides the truth to make us cross denominational lines. If you want the whole counsel of God, you can't get it in one particular group. The Baptists need to attend Pentecostal conventions; the charismatics, Presbyterian conventions.

Believe me, our world isn't impressed by the love of God just because we get up early on Sunday mornings and cram the kids into the car. They aren't persuaded by our big Bibles, political outbursts or our dogmatic opinions. Christianity will impress the world for one reason, and one reason alone:

> By THIS all will know that you are My disciples, IF you have love one for another.
>
> JOHN 13:35

I remember an old hymn that went something like this, "Lord, lay some soul upon my heart, and love that soul through me." One older gentleman, a natural soul winner, was asked to give his secret to successful evangelism.

He replied, "I love them until they ask me why!"

We could learn a great deal from that saint. Change is far more likely to occur in the lives of our porcupine people if we treat them with love and honor rather than criticism and disrespect.

A Christian is:
- The mind through which Jesus thinks.
- The heart through which Jesus loves.
- The voice through which Jesus speaks.
- The hand through which Jesus helps.

Being Loved Changes Behavior

Do you know what you get when you cross a pit bull with Lassie? You get a dog that will attack you and then run for help. Yes! A porcupine person may *hurt* you and then turn to help you later. Loving can trigger that transformation.

In the popular movie *Pretty Woman,* a man asks a prostitute why she ever got into the "world's oldest profession" (a misnomer that doesn't seem to take homemaking or motherhood into consideration). She explains that she is a runaway from an abusive home who, too ashamed to go home, now lives and works on the street.

Describing her first sexual encounter, she says, "One night I did it, and I cried the whole time. But it was the only way I found to survive."

Her would-be client somehow views her through different eyes at that point. He encourages her, saying, "You are too bright to do this; you have potential, you have special gifts."

The "pretty woman" is shocked; no one has ever believed in her before. She has been accustomed to thinking of herself as scum. As she gradually accepts this man's view of her, she begins to believe she is worth loving after all, too valuable to sell her body on the streets. She packs to leave her apartment and go back to school, turns to her roommate and says, "You are too good to do this; I believe you have potential—some special gifts."

Admittedly, the story is afflicted with an unlikely Hollywood plot. But the underlying principle is true: Love changes us. We love God because he first loved us. He initiated a process of spiritual transformation by seeing us through eyes of love. And, gradually, as we receive his grace, we are changed into more lovable and godly people.

Of course, there is an obvious responsibility in receiving God's love. We are, at his request, supposed to love others the way he loves us. That means we are to love them (like the Christian couple loved Julio) even when they aren't particularly lovable. Rather than risk raising their quills, why not try a love potion on them? Our love for them, our belief in them, our confidence in their strengths may or may not cause them to become the best people they can possibly be. But that isn't the point. We are to obey God's command because it is right, not use it to manipulate. Isn't that exactly the way God has made us into new people, "transformed by the renewing of your mind" (Rom 12:2)?

Praying For Our Enemies Changes Us

> Love your enemies ... pray for those who spitefully use you.
>
> MATTHEW 5:44

It has been said, "to understand is to forgive." As we love our enemies, we learn to pray for those who spitefully use us. In doing so, we discuss with God their circumstances and the possible reasons for their behavior. This kind of reflection allows us to be reminded of their difficulties, past hurts and disappointments. As we become aware of the likely reasons for their unpleasant behavior, we are better able to forgive their offenses. We find ourselves admitting,

- "Well, Lord, it's really sad. Caroline's mother never had time for her. She was left alone from the time she was a little girl. No wonder she takes care of number one. That's how she learned to survive."

- "You know, now that I think about it, my boss has been hurt by every woman who should have loved him. His mother walked out on him. His first wife had an affair and divorced him. His present wife talks to him like he's worthless. No wonder he's suspicious of me, so untrusting. He's probably suspicious of all females."

- "Father, I haven't always treated my daughter the way I should have. She's not very respectful of me, but maybe I haven't been as kind to her as I could have been, either. Her brother was always so much easier to handle."

Our prayers make spiritual provision for God to work in the lives of our porcupine people. But, perhaps even more profoundly, our prayers make it possible for God to soften our own hard hearts. Prayer gives us natural and supernatural understanding. Praying for our enemies changes relationships because it is virtually impossible to hate someone for whom we pray.

In the process of developing a loving attitude, I think you'll notice some interesting things happening within you. You will begin to know the life of God welling up within you.

> **W**e know that we have passed from death to life, because we love the brethren.
>
> 1 JOHN 3:14

No Love Means No Life

Love brings life. But the alternative can be deadly. Maybe you've met "Dissatisfied Diane." (There's at least one in every church.) Diane hasn't been around very long but is so disgruntled that soon she is sowing seeds of discord:

- "Well, that sermon sure left me cold this morning. I didn't get a thing out of it. Did you?"
- "The choir was good, but I think those new robes are too bright and distracting."
- "Did you hear the pastor's wife has taken a job at the hospital? I don't approve of pastors' wives working! It leads to all sorts of problems, if you know what I mean."

Chances are, if you checked Diane's track record you would find she's had many short stays in many churches. She is chronically discontent. Instead of dealing with her problem and learning how to love and be loving, she'd rather move on to a new group.

"Dissatisfied Diane" will inevitably make friends with "Bitter Betty." Like Diane, Betty didn't suddenly awake one morning and find bitterness had overtaken her in the night. A root of bitterness entrenched itself in her spirit over a period of time, growing on a daily basis, cultivated by an unloving and unforgiving spirit. It takes a progression of disappointments and subsequent withdrawals to nurture the poisonous plants we call dissatisfaction and bitterness. After a series of poor choices, Diane, Betty and others like them find themselves mistrustful of people in general. They develop a dark, cynical view of life.

I've noticed that when we close the door to loving, a window opens, and through it sweeps a cold draft that freezes us into rigidity and judgmentalism. Once, after returning to my house from the luxurious home of a wealthy friend, I began to look around with disdain at my furnishings. Before, I might have called them antiques, but now I could see that they were simply "junque." Suddenly I recognized that I needed new carpet. I needed a bigger guest room. I needed to paint the walls. The cold, negative wind of discontent began to blow through my heart. The moment I decided not to love what I had, it began to lose its value in my sight.

The same principle holds true if we decide to close the door to loving a spouse. We automatically, without realizing it, open the door to affection for someone else and become vulnerable to sexual attraction. Too many ex-spouses have the scars to prove this.

The risks we take by *not loving* far exceed those taken when we do love. They extend well beyond our houses and our spouses. There is solid medical evidence that a hard, bitter spirit endangers physical health. Positive, optimistic people consistently experience less stress, fewer illnesses and greater general health. Isn't a wholesome attitude well worth a dose of swallowed pride? Love brings life. It's good medicine!

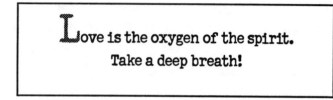

Love is the oxygen of the spirit.
Take a deep breath!

Choosing to Love Is an Act of Faith

After giving us the commandment to love in John's Gospel, Jesus gives us more reasons why we should keep it:

> I have spoken to you, that my joy may remain in you, and that your joy may be full.
>
> JOHN 15:11

Does that mean that if we love, everything will come out just the way we want? Look at it this way: Jesus was faced with a similar question. When he obeyed the Father's commandment to love, obedience was an act of supreme faith in his Father. He obeyed knowing that his love would be, for the most part, rejected. He saw in advance that his gifts of love would often not be received. He knew, even though he was the God of the universe, he would die on the cross to demonstrate unconditional love and to purchase salvation for you and me. But that wasn't the end of it. We read that Jesus, "For the joy set before Him endured the cross, despising the shame, and has sat down at the right hand of the throne of God" (Heb 12:2 NASB).

Jesus obeyed God's commandment to love because he believed the Father's promise of "the joy set before Him" (Heb 12:2 NASB). He believed that ultimately God would reward him richly for loving sacrifices. His faith was rewarded. Today he is seated "at the right hand of the throne of the Majesty in the heavens" (Heb 8:1). And someday, every knee will bow to Jesus, and every tongue confess that he is Lord (Phil 2:11).

But Jesus had to suffer in love to find his way into the promised joy. If Jesus was required to love, even though he knew his love would not be received graciously, how can we do less? Though we may experience disappointments, rejections, losses along the way, we have a wonderful assurance from God's Word that "all things work together for good to those who love God" (Rom 8:28). That means that our loving efforts are never lost, never poorly invested and never forgotten by God.

The Bible tells us in various passages, promises and parables that we will ultimately reap what we sow. Although love should never be given simply to manipulate some sort of reciprocation, sowing seeds of love will reap love, both in this life and in the life to come. Sowing seeds of love is not, of course, always done without pain. But God's Word talks to us about that kind of sowing and reaping.

Those who sow in tears shall reap with joyful shouting.
He who goes to and fro weeping, carrying his bag of seed,
Shall indeed come again with a shout of joy, bringing his sheaves with him.

PSALM 126:5-6 NASB

There are countless miracles of reconciliation, restoration and newly born love, and too many success stories for us to doubt God's ability to transform our most difficult relationships into testimonies of his power. But our faith should not be placed in some happy ending we've scripted in our imagination. Our faith should be in God's love for us.

> **L**ove is an act of faith because we believe in the Father's promises, in Jesus' example, and in the Holy Spirit's empowerment.

In eternity we won't need hope, wisdom, healing, prophecy or faith. Love will cross over, and we'll recognize and rejoice in seeing our loved ones, some of whom may have been the porcupine people we obediently decided to love no matter what.

Best of all, we will finally meet Jesus face to face—our example, our loving role model, the one who loved us unconditionally for a lifetime in spite of everything. Because of him we live, and love, and look forward to love's sweetest fruits, filling heaven with their fragrance. They will be abundantly ours forevermore.

That eternal outcome, dear friend, is God's generous reason for this powerful principle:

> **L**ove is not an option. Love is a commandment.

Reflections

1. What did Christ command (not suggest) his disciples to do?
2. How is it possible to fulfill all the laws of God?
3. What is to be the sign to the world of the love of God in Christ Jesus?
4. How can we avoid becoming a disgruntled and bitter person?
5. Name at least two benefits Jesus promised to those who are learning to love.
6. Take a moment to pledge yourself to pray for your difficult person right now. Mention him or her by name out loud. Tell the Lord you intend to begin to sow love into that person, trusting in his power to enable you.

THREE

Enemies: You Gotta Love 'Em!

Take a few minutes and try to honestly answer the following questions:

- Could you make friends with an outspoken "left-wing" neighbor?
- Do you write off women whose worldviews are less traditional than yours as "feminazis" or "anti-family-values"?
- Do you feel angry about, or afraid of, homosexuals?
- Have you become annoyed with the secular media?
- Could you befriend an atheist?

> **Definition of Atheist:**
> a person with no
> invisible means of support.

What does it mean to be a loving person? How are we to love the people we love to hate? Is it possible to love the sinner while hating the sin? Learning to cultivate love in our lives means believing in a God of love who can impart love to us and through us, even for our porcupine people. Sounds good, doesn't it? Unfortunately, in some cases, it's easier said than done.

God Loves You and I'm Trying

I'd like to overlook it, joke about it or just pretend it's not there. But I can't. The truth is, I am grieved by the lack of love I see demonstrated by churchgoing friends. Too many churches have their share of members who would rather nit-pick than reach out. These people seem to enjoy emphasizing negatives, judging others and lifting themselves into a position of authority over those who fall short of their ideals.

Pharisees are always looking for a sign of God's punishment—or, rather, God's punishment of someone besides themselves. They simply do not recognize the truth behind the idea that rain falls on the just and the unjust. They cannot comprehend that bad things do happen to good people. When hearing of a tragedy, these individuals intrude by asking if, "just maybe," there might be sin in the life of the victim. In Jesus' day, they even brought a blind man before him, inquiring, "Who sinned—this man or his parents, that he was born blind?"

Jesus was irritated with them and responded, "Neither this man nor his parents sinned, but that the works of God should be revealed in him ..." (Jn 9:3). He concluded his comments by healing the blind man on the spot.

We have more than our share of Pharisees two thousand years after Jesus took them on. They are in our churches, Christian organizations and everywhere else the gospel is preached. These "professional Christian hit men" or "God's snipers," ready to shoot down any suspicious person who steps out of line, seem to come with the territory. Let's not negotiate with these "terrorists for Christ." Some of them make a career of critical thinking. When I compare their judgmental attitudes with the standard of love that God set, my heart sinks.

Called to love, we should never be caught refusing to love someone just because he or she doesn't agree with us. For that matter, we should not refuse to love those who disagree with God, defy him or deny his existence. It's worth noting that in the kingdom of God there are no undercover agents. Author Jamie Buckingham used to say,

> There is a thin line between muckraking and solid analysis. That line is called love.

Love Across Denominational Differences

The fact that denominations are diverse does not mean that all Christians are divided, any more than conformity makes us automatically unified. But we should ask ourselves: *Who rubs me the wrong way? Which preacher's style turns me off? Are there certain groups whose doctrines are a bit too far out for my liking? Are there congregations who are too demonstrative or too conservative in their worship for my taste?* If you can't see that someone's way of doing things matches Scripture, perhaps you don't know all there is to know about Scripture. Even if you're right, does that mean you can't love them anyway?

> A religious argument is an oxymoron.

I am grateful for the wonderful truths God seems to have spread generously among our myriad Christian denominations. These variations are there to help us all step across invisible lines and force us to come together to get the full picture of God. I am grateful for the much bigger picture I have of God that was gained by embracing truths held sacred by different denominational camps.

I've been deeply immersed in Baptist churches since my conversion at a Billy Graham crusade. I have learned through the beautiful doctrinal truths of the Lutherans and Presbyterians about the sovereignty of God: predestination, election and calling. Much of my knowledge of God has been enhanced and expanded through the charismatic experience. And my conversations and friendships with Roman Catholic believers have brought me to a respect of their sense of God's mystery, the communion of saints and the rich symbolism in their worship. God is so big! We need to gain an understanding of him as both Spirit and Truth, subjective and objective, in order to continue to move toward maturity in Christ.

> All truth? You dry up.
> All spirit? You blow up.
> Spirit and truth? You grow up!

Consider the theology of the sovereignty of God, which encompasses the wonderful doctrines of election, predestination and calling. Contrast those truths with human free will. If we choose to focus solely on the sovereignty doctrine, to the exclusion of man's free will, we can find ourselves blasé about evangelism, thinking, *Well, if God's going to get them saved anyway, he'll get the work done without my help!* But a doctrinal emphasis solely on the responsibility of people, with the urgency and need for everyone to come to Christ, can make you a crazed evangelist, accosting anything that moves. Free-will teaching needs to be tempered with a sense of God's sovereignty.

Which teaching is right? They both are. We encounter paradoxes every day. We say, "He who hesitates is lost." We also say, "Look before you leap." Both are true, when applied to specific situations. God's truths are so magnificent that they can only be fully realized in the form of paradox through love.

"No virtue is really a virtue unless it is permeated by love," writes Richard McBrient, who outlines some of the pitfalls of doctrinal correctness:

> *Justice without love is legalism.*
> *Faith without love is ideology.*
> *Hope without love is self-centeredness.*
> *Forgiveness without love is self-abasement.*
> *Fortitude without love is recklessness.*
> *Generosity without love is extravagance.*
> *Care without love is obligation.*
> *Fidelity without love is servitude.*[1]

Loving Cults and Anti-Cults Into Truth

After terrible episodes like the Heaven's Gate suicides and the Branch Davidian tragedy in Waco, Texas, we are reminded of the strange religious groups that sometimes rise up. These groups frustrate and frighten us, and sometimes we want to lash out, particularly when we see them seductively recruiting young people into their ranks.

In our efforts to uphold truth, we can become so opinionated about those who distort and discard Scripture that we cease to simply accept them as human beings. Cultists are often fearful individuals who are social misfits. A sense of community and self-empowerment most likely drew them into a cult in the first place. What makes us think our rejection of them will make them inclined to turn to Christ? Excluding and ostracizing them only reinforces their commitment to the cult.

Even after leaving a cult, many cling to small groups of "ex-cultists" and continue their defensive, combative thinking. They turn their attention toward fighting the cult rather than seeking peace, leaving their past behind them and growing in the Christian community. Only our love over the long haul will draw them in.

Behind Enemy Lines

Some people are so concerned with being politically correct that they lose all individual identity and begin to look and sound alike. I wonder if some of our Christian "values-centered" correctness may leave the Church with just such a tendency to clone. It is appropriate for us to dislike certain messages, but we must still cultivate love for the messenger.

I've seen Christian activists waving their Bibles, holding up signs that say "God hates fags" and screaming at homosexuals in gay rights parades. I've watched taunting crowds of believers locked in arguments with abortion-rights activists outside clinics. Are their motives right? Probably. Biblically motivated folks get all fired up about unrighteousness. But are their methods right? I doubt it!

> People who fight fire with fire usually end up with nothing but ashes.

I understand the frustration of "family values" folks. We are scoffed at and scorned as the "radical religious right." We can easily find ourselves caught in heated arguments over prayer in school, pornography and other political, cultural and moral issues on which we stand. How easily we might be viewed as just another angry, disagreeable mob. We're mad about the liberal media, militant movements, raw movies, the ACLU, educational issues, crime and any number of other concerns. But angry arguments rarely settle issues and often leave hurt feelings, bitterness and harsh resentment in their wake. Is that what we want to accomplish? When I speak before a group of politically active Christians, I encourage them not to forget love.

It's all too easy to paint ourselves into a corner along with those who are ticked off at the leadership in the White House, those raging at the local school board members, or any number of other polarized groups. We feel the frustration of being behind the power curve in our culture, rejected for positions of leadership and influence. Our very orthodoxy can cause us to acquire a distorted and negative view of our country. I realized what an unloving attitude I had developed when I talked with a Christian friend who faithfully prays for our country's leaders. It dawned on me that she was praying for the people I was praying against.

> It's hard to become a more loving person if you don't LIKE people to begin with.

In his thoughtful booklet *Loving Those We'd Rather Hate*, Joseph Stowell makes us rethink some things: "I fear that looking at some of us within the church of Christ today, it would be hard to see that we are on a seek-and-save mission since we look so much more like we're into search-and-destroy! We must not permit our fiery faith to drain our compassion!"[2]

Humble Thyself in the Sight of the Lord

Most people in Norma McCorvey's hometown knew her real name. But as "Jane Roe" she had played a significant part in the media reports regarding *Roe v. Wade*, the U.S. Supreme Court decision in 1973. Her lie about being gang-raped and subsequently unable to get an abortion ignited the pro-life/pro-choice debate in America. But as McCorvey walked to her car one evening after work, she encountered Philip Benham, the director of a nearby Operation Rescue headquarters.

Philip screamed at Norma, "Your lie opened the door to the slaughter of thirty-five million children! You should be ashamed!"[3] McCorvey didn't feel shame at that moment. She felt shock and anger.

Later, Philip was troubled about the way he had shouted. He went to McCorvey and humbly apologized for the unloving way he had delivered the message. This display of humility so touched her that McCorvey began to visit Benham at the Operation Rescue office. Her attitude changed. Eventually she came to comprehend the full extent of her actions. She received God's love and forgiveness in Jesus Christ. Today, she is a growing believer, active in the pro-life movement.

It wasn't information that changed McCorvey. It wasn't argument. It wasn't rage. It was love and humility—the qualities Jesus required of those who follow him.

Where There's Smoke

Speaking of humility, how do you respond to people who smoke? Do you become angry and defensive when you see them light up a cigarette? Or are you able to allow them to pursue their unhealthy habit without feeling obligated to communicate your disapproval? Many adult smokers long to stop smoking but have not yet found the strength to do so. They feel marginalized by the new nonsmoking rules and are often sensitive to the discomfort of those around them. Instead of speaking self-righteously or looking down on them, try asking them nicely to move or to extinguish their smokes.

> **W**ould Jesus request a seat in the nonsmoking section?

Is Something Missing?

What evidence did Jesus tell us will prove to the world that we are disciples of his? Is it evident in your life? I ask myself the same question, imagining the Divine Courtroom now, with Judge John presiding. He bangs his gavel in finality: "This court has found too little evidence to convict the accused of being a Christian. The witnesses have only given circumstantial evidence, not admissible in the courtroom. We recognize church attendance, a car sporting Christian bumper stickers, certain righteous deeds, humanitarian efforts and theological studies. But this court is charged to judge by only one rule: 'By THIS all will know that you are my disciples; IF you have love for one another' (Jn 13:35). There is simply not enough evidence in the accused's life to support the charge. Case dismissed."

> **I**f you were accused of being a Christian, would there be enough evidence to convict you?

Vitally important qualities are missing in the expression of Christian faith in today's world. Where is the Church of Christ identifiable by her compassion, grace and mercy? Christ taught his disciples not to focus on the decadence of the Roman society in which they lived. After all, the best humankind can do without the Spirit of God is to live out the fallen nature we all inherited from Adam and Eve. The Lord's followers were to see beyond this, to view people lovingly—as lost folks, people who were simply doing what comes naturally. Jesus had the power and right to rally the world into a revolution against the pagan powers of his day; he could have called down angelic platoons to carry out his orders. But Jesus had a greater priority: to reach human beings who were separated from his heavenly Father. He told us he came not to condemn the world but to save it (see Jn 3:17).

> He has shown you, O man, what is good;
> And what does the Lord require of you
> But to do justly,
> To love mercy,
> And to walk humbly with your God?
>
> MICAH 6:8

This image from Micah is a perfect picture of Jesus, who walked humbly with God, did justice and loved kindness. Jesus was passionately addicted to mercy. He lived out his earthly life in an unjust society, was wrongly accused, tortured and murdered, yet cried out from the cross, "Father, forgive them, for they do not know what they do" (Lk 23:34). Aren't we to be conformed to the image of Christ? Do we have this loving public image, or do we appear to be another disgruntled, disenfranchised group, enraged about losing political power and clout?

I'm not saying that we who have deep religious convictions

should bury our heads in the sand. I believe we should be involved in the political process and the issues that affect the future of this nation. My husband, Hal, and I are publicly identified as conservative (we believe Jesus rode into Jerusalem on an elephant, not a donkey) due largely to Hal's service with the Commission of Immigration for the Western Region of the United States during the Ronald Reagan administration. But Hal and I continually examine ourselves, careful to assure we don't become so outspoken politically that we alienate ourselves. Each of us must keep asking if we have positioned ourselves as enemies or view the other camp as enemies. If so, then we must remember what Jesus wants us to do: *Love your enemies* (Mt 5:44).

We may choose to distance ourselves from others whose values oppose ours, but Jesus went straight after them. He chose to be with them. He ate and drank with them. He fished with them. His goal was to seek and to save that which was lost. He did not come to comfort the saved ones. He did not come simply to reform the behavior of the lost. He came to change men and women from within by the power of the Holy Spirit. He's still doing it today.

The Church is not a museum for saints. It is a hospital for sinners!

Reflections

1. How is your experience with God one of Spirit as well as Truth? Why not ask God for the infilling of the Holy Spirit so you can "know him and the power of his resurrection" (Phil 3:10) in greater measure?

2. Are you willing to give the benefit of the doubt to a brother or sister in Christ? Although their interpretation of biblical truth may differ from yours, why not focus on what you share (the thing that unites you) rather than the thing that divides you?

3. What political or social groups do you consider "enemy camp"? Do you want to be a positive example of God's love to them, rather than a representative of his wrath? Choose to cultivate love and understanding.

FOUR

Relationships:
The Ties That Bind (and Gag)

Lorraine looked across the table at her mother. Oddly, the first thing she noticed was the older woman's hands. Wrinkled and spotted with age, they moved constantly, the fingers opening and closing nervously. Lorraine felt a surge of guilt. *Those are the same hands that changed my diapers when I was a baby,* she reminded herself, feeling a little weepy. *They sewed my clothes. They dried my tears.*

Just then another memory came into view in the daughter's mind. *Yeah, they whacked me a few times, too.* The recollection of some of her mother's firmly applied spankings made Lorraine feel a little less nostalgic.

Lorraine and her husband, Jack, had made a place for Edith in their home just a year before. Until that time, mother and daughter had gotten along well. They'd talked on the phone nearly every day, shopped together, lunched at favorite restaurants and gossiped relentlessly, sometimes reflecting about how sad it was that other mothers and daughters didn't enjoy one another. Within months of Edith's move, however, the relationship between the two women changed dramatically.

Lorraine quickly became convinced that, in her mother's eyes, she couldn't do anything right. Edith seemed to have focused her capacity for "constructive criticism" solely on her daughter, unaware of its effect on Lorraine. Actually, Edith thought Lorraine was a wonderful person. As a mother, she felt she was simply offering "a few suggestions" now and then. It made her feel like she was making a contribution. While regretting the fact she had become a burden in her golden years, Edith couldn't understand why Lorraine was giving her the cold shoulder. Her daughter's silence was a mystery, leaving her feeling lost and confused.

Edith and Lorraine virtually stopped talking to each other. Each was afraid to hurt the other by opening a conversation about the difficulties between them. Each was equally afraid to hear what the other might have to say. Lorraine was preparing to ask her mother to move out while Edith was living in regret that she'd agreed to sell her house. Might a decision to love again rescue the severely strained relationship between this mother and daughter? Fortunately, before all was lost, that's exactly the decision the two women made.

What about you? Take an honest inventory. Are you making a genuine attempt to love the porcupine people in your life? Ask yourself a few pointed, even prickly, questions:

- Do you and your spouse find more to fight about than to enjoy together?
- Have you cut yourself off from a son or daughter who irritates you?
- Are you avoiding an intolerable person at work? Are you avoiding anyone?

- Does conversation with one or both of your parents end up in a hot argument or a cold chill?
- Has silence replaced conversation between you and someone you once enjoyed?
- Does a person who once delighted you now drive you up the wall?
- Do you feel victimized by someone?
- Are you unsure which relationships in your life should be salvaged and which scrapped?

Did Someone Say, "Love Thy Neighbor"?

Maybe you've asked yourself, *just who am I supposed to be learning to love again?* You can't exactly love everybody, can you? Jesus answered this question by telling his disciples a story that does not leave much room for maneuvering *around* porcupine people.

I imagine the kindhearted hero of Jesus' story would never have guessed his nickname would become forever "The Good Samaritan." In fact, this man was just another decent fellow going about his business. But everything changed when he came across another man lying on the side of the road, the victim of a mugging. The bruised and battered man had been passed by many others during the course of the day. "Sam" came by, the Bible says, and "when he saw him, he had compassion" (Lk 10:33). Sam picked him up and took care of him.

The story is ancient, but its message is up-to-date. It provides us with a good "love gauge." Who are we are supposed to love? According to Jesus, we are to love anyone we encounter who deserves our compassion. It may be someone who lives nearby, or (as in Sam's case) it may simply be someone who comes into physical proximity. Jesus' command refers to anyone who is close enough for us to care about: a cashier at a gas station, a postal worker, a fellow employee or someone at church, maybe even the preacher.

What Is This Thing Called Love?

Sometimes our problem loving porcupine people involves over-optimistic expectations about the way we're supposed to *feel*. One of the difficulties is the word love itself. What exactly is meant by that? Is love an obligation? An obsession? A worshipful obeisance? Should we be experiencing chills and warm fuzzies?

When I was involved in musical comedy theater work, I had the opportunity to perform in *Fiddler on the Roof* at the Crystal Cathedral in California. I played the coveted role of Golde, a manipulating Jewish mama (and heaven knows, I was well typecast). Tevye (Golde's husband) and I sang together about love:

Tevye: "Golde ... do you *love* me?"

Golde: "Do I LOVE you? For twenty-five years I've washed your clothes, cooked your meals, cleaned your house, given you children, milked the cow. After twenty-five years why talk about love right now?"

Tevye: "But my father and my mother said we'd learn to love each other, and now I'm asking, 'Golde, do you *love* me?'"

Golde: (to the audience) "For twenty-five years I lived with him, fought with him, starved with him, for twenty-five years my bed is his. If that's not love, what is?"[1]

Fiddler on the Roof provides a resoundingly true and touching portrait of love. But it is an exception to the messages we receive from so many films, songs, novels and other fantasies reflected by today's media-mad world. Worldly portrayals of love confuse, constrict and convolute our ideas about what love is and what we should expect from it. Love occasionally offers us emotional highs, which are wonderful and unforgettable. But in fact, those highs are few and far between. The real day-in-day-out effects of love are courtesy, consideration, sacrifice, generosity and kindness. Whether our porcupine people live under our roof or not, love should make them feel welcome in our presence, aware of our unconditional affection and unrelenting commitment to their well-being. Sound like *Mission: Impossible*?

According to God's Word, it isn't impossible. How do I know that? Because Titus 2:4 instructs us to "admonish the young women to love their husbands." If we are able to teach one another to love, then love is within our reach. And learning to love porcupine people is within our grasp.

Check Your Receiver

Lorraine and Edith, the mother and daughter we met earlier in the chapter, both felt unloved. The mother believed the daughter had stopped loving her, and vice versa. The reality was, they were both wrong. They had each allowed fears of failure, hurt feelings and misconceptions to eclipse the love they still cherished for each other. They had merely stopped communicating.

If you are the proud owner of a nonconfrontational personality, you've probably heard yourself say, "When people make me mad, I think the best thing to do is to shut up before things escalate." That may seem like a peaceable solution, but it is the worst possible plan. Love doesn't mean clam up. It means open up. Love requires toleration, confrontation and vulnerability in the context of endless conversation. People who love aren't defensive. They have open ears and are not driven away when they hear less-than-complimentary comments about themselves. Successful lovers care more about others than about their own self-esteem.

> **L**oving a porcupine requires thick skin and a soft heart.

Life may have convinced you that you are not loved anymore by the person from whom you most want love. Feeling unloved is not an unusual reaction. But consider this possibility: that person may be transmitting love. The problem may be that you and she or he are on different wavelengths!

- Your teenager may be transmitting love through her bursts of anger—it matters so much to her to be close to you, and she's frustrated by all the misunderstandings.

- Your toddler's tantrum may be communicating that he is jealous because you are spending time (away from him) on the telephone—he loves you so much he wants you all to himself.
- Your friend's silence may be a loving cry for help—"Please ask me what's wrong," she's saying, "I'm too afraid to tell you."
- Your boyfriend may be keeping his distance because he's feeling more and more in love with you and (no surprise here, ladies) he's afraid to make a permanent commitment.
- Your husband's habit of working long hours may be his way of showing love and care for the family by trying to make more money.

My husband and I are genuine opposites, and this means we're often on different wavelengths. From my perspective, Hal would be demonstrating love if he were to bring home a handful of flowers (other than from the front yard). But to him, flowers aren't love, they're a waste of money. To me, romance includes a warm, crackling fireplace. Hal says, "This is hot; how can you stand this?" To me, love means *presents*. Hal agrees with that all right; he says, "When I come home, you have my *presence!*"

Love … in Spite of Everything Else

Sometimes love requires us to do the most difficult thing imaginable. Jill and Bob made a mutual decision to divorce and share custody of their kids. Through all the hassles of settlements and other issues, Bob had long since lost that loving feeling for Jill. Or had he? In his quiet moments, he had to admit that "something" was still there. And that something bothered him.

Jill wasn't bothered at all. She quickly trimmed down, polished up her nails along with her dating skills and began to play the field. Before long, Bob was struggling not only with rejection but with jealousy, so he began to pray about his ever-growing bad attitude. He soon felt God gave him an idea—and it wasn't a welcome one.

Bob knew Jill's biggest struggle was getting a sitter for their two small children so she could pursue her newfound freedom. *Offer to baby-sit,* the thought came into his mind.

Offer to baby-sit! the thought persisted. All his arguments about why that was not a good idea wouldn't compute. After two weeks, Bob called Jill and asked if she could use his help with the kids that week.

"You must be joking," she said slowly.

"No, not really. Baby sitters are tough to get during the week. So tell me what night is good for you."

Bob arranged to go over to the house Wednesday night but regretted it the minute he drove the car into the driveway. "This is emotional suicide!" he prayed. "I'm only doing it to try to be obedient to you, Lord."

The house felt like home—too much like home—as he offered the kids the McDonald's Happy Meals he brought with him. But when Jill's date walked through the door, he was put to the supreme test.

"Your ex is baby-sitting for us?" the stranger said to Jill, giving Bob a sly wink. "Hey, thanks a lot."

Gross, Bob thought. *I must be a real sucker.* But as the night wore on, Bob had the most meaningful talk ever with his nine-year-old son. For once, it seemed they got below the surface and experienced some healing. When Jill returned home around midnight, she and Bob said little.

The second time Bob baby-sat, Jill couldn't resist asking, "Why are you doing this?"

"Because I care about the kids—and you," Bob answered. "I want to help out. I was a jerk too much of the time we were married. Maybe I can make up for a little of it now."

Jill looked shocked, reached for her purse over the kitchen counter, then left with a puzzled look on her face. When she returned, she was full of questions. For the first time in years, their conversation seemed to reach beyond the usual complaints and arguments.

Have they remarried? No. Not yet, anyway. But something wonderful has happened in Bob. Because of his decision to show love (even when it was barely there), he pleased the Lord. In response, God has given him a new sense of peace that is nothing short of supernatural. Bob chose to love rather than react. And he was wise. The feeling of dreading Jill's phone calls is gone, and the sharp words between them have faded away.

What Love Isn't

"Lee, I've got to talk to you about my husband."

"Excuse me, Mrs. Ezell. I'd like to ask you a question. See, there's this man …"

"Oh, Lee, I'm so in love, and I'm so miserable! What can I do?"

Ever since I started speaking to women's groups, I've discovered there is one form of love so common, even among mature women, that I think it deserves a few comments. I'm talking about relationship addiction.

"Man junkies," as I call them, are women who are strung out on their need for romance and the yearning to be with somebody, no matter who or what. Many would-be good relationships are sabotaged by this kind of private obsession. Being hooked on a man has the power both to destroy good marriages and to hold destructive marriages together. Although no chemical substance is involved, man junkies are just as dependent on their relationships as heroin addicts are on their drug.

Although relationship addiction usually involves male-female liaisons, it is not limited to mixed-sex couples. An unhealthy relationship can develop between best friends of the same sex who become possessive, jealous and exclusive. A parent may become obsessed with her child, smothering instead of mothering. An addictive relationship can also develop between a spiritual leader and a follower, a boss and an employee—in almost any kind of association, close or distant. Often one who becomes hooked on a person displays a pattern of a lifetime of unhealthy relationships with both family and friends.

But is this love? Relationship addiction is actually an emotion-backed demand. It is a way of using the other person to supply something we feel we need. Attachment arises out of our own incompleteness rather than out of concern for the other person. We mistake it for love, but it's something far less desirable. It is essential to ask ourselves, when we are trying to "fix" an uncomfortable or unrewarding relationship, just what it is we are trying to accomplish. Love is not a desperate attempt to attach ourselves to another person in order to escape our own neediness.

> **Am I trying to love a person or to recapture an elusive feeling?**

That brings me to another important point, that is, a word of warning. Another thing love is *not*: it is not tolerant of abuse. No matter how much we may want to love a porcupine person, we are not required to put up with abuse, physical or emotional assault or mistreatment from our children. It is ignorant—not loving—for a woman, man or child to remain silent in an abusive relationship. Sometimes we confuse certain intense feelings with love. Because of family background or other painful circumstance, some people equate love with sick feelings of fear, neediness, anxiety, jealousy or heartache. Illogical longings that keep us going back to abusive or addictive behavior are not loving emotions but symptoms of "enabling" or "codependent" behavior. They indicate behavior patterns and issues of love that should be taken up with a wise counselor.

> **warning:**
> If you are hungry for love you
> will eat any kind of garbage.

"I'm Not Sure I Ever Loved Him"

Do you sometimes wonder if you ever really loved that difficult person in the first place? Pain and resentment can blur memories, creating a kind of angry amnesia that refuses to remember the good times. If that's part of your problem, take heart. Look at it this way: instead of trying to renovate something old, you now have the opportunity to build something new. As you work toward reconciliation, create the best relationship possible from original raw materials. Love is not a matter of counting the years. It's a matter of making the years count.

Think about your spiritual life for a moment. Forget the missionary donations you've made. Forget the street-corner evangelism. Forget the Christian lyrics you've memorized, the verses you can quote, the sermon tapes you've passed around, the tithe checks you've written. Instead of all that, think about your last encounter with your porcupine person. Love is the litmus test of the Christian life. When you last saw that person, how did you act? What did you say? What impression did you make?

If your answer to that question ranges from "Could you give me a minute to think it over?" to "I'm not sure," to "No way, José!" consider the seven steps toward reconciliation found in Part II. There's no time like the present and nothing more important in the course of a lifetime than people. We can leave them, loathe them or love them. Our Lord has commanded us to love them; the choice is ours.

God is not trying to get us into heaven. God is trying to get heaven into us!

Reflections

1. Write down the reasons you feel you've lost love for some porcupine person. Describe your present reactions to him or her.
2. How do truth and the work of the Holy Spirit combine in your efforts to love unlovely people?
3. Define love the way you'd like to give and receive it.
4. Can you think of ways you might have misinterpreted your porcupine person's behavior? Explain.
5. How can you tell the difference between love and relationship addiction?
6. Write your thoughts about why God commands us to love one another.

Part II

The ABCs of Loving Again

FIVE

A=Accept Them ...
Just As They Are

Joyce and Tom sat in their backyard, taking a breather after a difficult day. They had always been committed to Christian parenting but now were talking about their struggle with feelings of guilt involving their teenager.

Just then their daughter marched out through the back door. "Look," she announced, "I know you don't like Dave, but I want to warn you—in two weeks I'll be eighteen, and I am going to marry him, no matter what you say, with or without your blessing, in Vegas or in church. You either accept him into the family or kiss me goodbye!" With that, the door slammed.

Joyce and Tom looked at each other in silence. Ouch! It seemed they were left with two unpalatable choices: accept the disgusting boy their daughter had dragged home or lose her altogether. No way was Dave the husband they had diligently prayed for. Even positive thinking wouldn't help at this point, à la "at least his tattoos are all spelled right." Nope. There was no way to put an upbeat spin on this one!

How were Joyce and Tom to accept this young man? What about their spiritual standards? Could they let their daughter be unequally yoked with a blatant unbeliever? What about the two younger kids? Perhaps they were thinking, *Wow, our parents are rad! You can drag home any old garbage, and they'll say fine.*

Joyce and Tom set out to poll their Christian friends for advice but didn't find much help there, either. Everybody they asked gave them a different opinion. Finally, they asked the most loving man they knew, who smiled knowingly and replied, "Well, it's quite simple, isn't it? If you want to walk with Jesus, you must walk in love. But, of course, if you don't want to walk with Jesus, just reject his commandment to walk in love, and walk in darkness."

The truth of those words pierced their hearts. Joyce and Tom began their journey down the road less traveled. The struggling parents began asking their daughter's boyfriend to come over and watch TV with them. (They avoided saying, "Oh, sure! We'd love to have you put some more cigarette burn holes in our furniture.") When the Christmas season rolled around, they decided to buy him a gift.

Something was happening. Joyce and Tom couldn't figure out if it was just their perception or if the boy's behavior was beginning to change. They began to see that under a rough exterior was a gentle kid who needed understanding. They also noticed that Dave was showing up less frequently at their house—and calling less for their daughter. Haltingly Mom inquired, "How come we didn't see much of Dave this week?"

The girl flippantly replied: "Oh, I'm off Dave now. I have a new boyfriend. He's coming over tonight."

Mom wanted to scream, "What? After all you've put us through?" Fortunately, she didn't.

> Other people do not have to change for me to love them; I have to change for me to love them.

Accept the Value in Being Human

You've heard it a thousand times: love them unconditionally. Sounds easy, right? But those of us who have honestly tried to do so realize the difficulty. One way of motivating unconditional acceptance is to reflect upon the value God places upon every human being. Each of us is valuable simply because God says we are. We are also valuable because before the foundation of the world he designed each of us uniquely.

A quick read of Psalm 139 reminds us of every person's wonderful place in God's creation. In fact, God thought the human race was so valuable that he sent his Son to die for it (more about that later). Each of us has further value because God has purposes for us. He is able and willing to employ every person alive—believers and unbelievers alike—to accomplish his great plans.

If we accept others simply because of their value as human beings, the way God does—not based on achievements or performance—our job becomes easier. The behaviors and attitudes that trouble us are instantly removed from the equation. We do not evaluate porcupine people because of what they do or do not do. We find value in them simply because God placed them in the world and in our lives for his own reasons.

Because we honor God and respect his great plan for our lives, we accept others exactly where they are, whether or not we like their behavior, opinions, appearance, choices and failures. This has helped me especially when I looked at my children's rebellious behavior and said to myself, "This is their present orientation," while clinging to the hope, "This too shall pass." Acceptance does not mean living in denial about unpleasant realities. Neither does acceptance allow despair to overtake us.

> **My task is to ACCEPT others, not to APPROVE others.**

We must surrender the idea of rejecting certain people because they are not living up to their potential. With vain imaginations, we tend to carve an image of what another person should or could be and then withhold acceptance while waiting for that perfect individual to emerge. Until this fairy-tale person magically appears (after all, we've prayed, haven't we?), we make an unconscious decision not to accept anything less. This kind of mental image-making needs to stop because, as long as we entertain it, we'll never be satisfied with anybody.

When Did God Accept Us?

Most of us sincerely desire to fulfill Christ's command to love one another but need to examine the "as I have loved you" portion of that concept. Somewhere, before the foundations of the earth were laid, God made a decision to love and accept you and me. "God so loved the world that he gave his only begotten Son ..." (Jn 3:16) was determined way before he saw whether we deserved it or not. Because he set the example first, God can tell us to love one another in the same abandoned, unconditional way. As God accepts me, he expects me to accept others and myself. Believers should gladly follow suit, loving prickly people whether we think they deserve love or not. How else is God going to be able to show his unconditional love to the world if not through us? He has chosen us to be his hands, his feet, his eyes, his lips and his heart of compassion.

Think of all the embarrassing things God has accepted about you and me: our stubbornness, unfaithfulness, quick tempers, lack of discipline, ingratitude. Once you've taken that little inventory, don't you want to thank him for the way he has blessed you, warts and all? Doesn't that make it easier for you to thank him for your porcupine people? After thanking God for putting that specially challenging person in your life, try this: ask God to help arrange a time and an appropriate way for you to tell that person that you accept them just as they are—no changes necessary.

God loved us before we desired or deserved it!

I recently saw a video about a young man who experienced Christian love and acceptance in a way that genuinely saved his life. Raul was a "drag queen," a male prostitute on the streets of Los Angeles. He arrived as a teenager seeking fame in Hollywood, soon becoming addicted to heroin. In the throes of his addiction, he was sexually assaulted by men and eventually set up by a pimp to earn his drugs by soliciting male sex partners. Raul grew his hair long and bleached it blond. The massive doses of female hormones he took made him appear as a sensual woman. Although he often went hungry and homeless in the daytime, each night found him making about $500, most of which went to his pimp.

Raul later said, "I always knew that God loved me, but I never felt accepted as a man. And I never met a man who could love me in the right way."

Finally, a Christian man decided to accept Raul exactly the way he was. He befriended him and invited him to attend a meeting at his inner-city church. Raul objected. Considering his appearance, he was too embarrassed to show up.

"Not a problem," his new friend insisted, assuring Raul that he would be accepted among the other churchgoers. After a great deal of convincing, the confused young man attended a service.

Raul told his friend that he'd like to attend services regularly but added, "I don't want to just cut my hair and change my clothes. I would still feel like a woman. I have to be changed inside, in order to change on the outside. I tried before, you know, but this thing was stronger than me."

The next time Raul returned to church, he accepted Christ as his Savior. His life changed forever. From that time on, he worked at changing himself, inside and out. He asked his friend to help him find male clothing and sought advice about styling his hair. The more he felt the acceptance of other

Christians, the more open he was to a dramatic lifestyle change.

The love and acceptance of both God and God's people have entirely transformed Raul, who is struggling with AIDS today but is happily married. The brother who made the commitment to accept him also assisted Raul as he found his way into drug rehab, where he was delivered from his addiction to heroin.

Acceptance or Approval?

Acceptance is an expression of love. Approval is not. It would have been disastrous for Raul's Christian friend to say "Hey, Raul, just stay the way you are. I think you're terrific." Raul needed to change. His life depended on it. In fact, there are several reasons to avoid confusing acceptance with approval.

"If love and approval are essentially the same in my mind," writes Rich Buhler, "then it will seem logical to go on a 'love strike' as a way of communicating my dissatisfaction with something in another person."[1] Buhler goes on to explain that if we confuse acceptance with approval there are at least three possible consequences.

First, we may tend to withhold love as a way of expressing our disapproval. This often happens between parents and children. If the child misbehaves, mom or dad becomes angry and refuses a good night kiss or hug. Sometimes the cold shoulder continues for days while the child is left with the impression the parent no longer loves her (or him) because of misbehavior. Or a wife might refuse to make love to her husband because she disapproves of something he has done (or hasn't remembered to do!). A man, in turn, may refuse to communicate with his wife for similar reasons; through the silent treatment, he thinks he is teaching her a lesson.

Second, we may interpret disapproval as a withdrawal of love and acceptance. Men and women who grew up in homes where love had to be earned are susceptible to this. Criticism, reproof, or disagreement feels like rejection and can result in angry defensiveness or depression that far exceeds an appropriate response. The overreaction of such people often takes their critics by surprise, causing them to think twice before communicating anything remotely suggestive of change.

Third, if we confuse acceptance with approval, we will grant others approval as a means of trying to give them love. This can lead to overlooking bad habits, enabling addictive behavior and refusing to confront inappropriate, hurtful actions. When we misunderstand acceptance, we do not know how to communicate our needs or desires about others' behavior without a deep fear of damaging the relationship. We may be tempted to accept the unacceptable in a porcupine person because we want them to be happy in our company. Confrontation always involves periods of unpleasantness, and it scares us to risk further alienation. It may help to remember that making someone else happy is as impossible as negating the calories in a slice of chocolate cake by washing it down with a can of Diet Coke!

Acceptance Doesn't Guarantee Change

If you aren't quite willing to accept folks just as they are, consider the options. Total rejection is one, of course, but not a loving choice. What about trying to change the other person? Suppose you come up with a master scheme, including superficial acceptance, in order to manipulate them, send them on a first-class guilt trip or otherwise engineer some miracle cure? Unfortunately, the very most that all your psychological tricks will produce is only temporary change.

In refusing to accept people the way they are, you are saying:

- I will love you if you please me.
- I will care for you when (and if) you live right.
- When you please God, you'll please me.
- Your behavior is more important than you are.
- I know more about who and what you are supposed to be than you do.

Do these attitudes lead to change? No, usually they create very much the opposite response: further separation, rebellion and estrangement. The fact is, try as you might, God never gave one person the power—or the right—to change another. There is no such spiritual gift. Even fasting and praying for forty days and forty nights can't provide that kind of power. But there's good news, too:

> **W**here you feel you have no control, you probably have no responsibility.

Clearly, you are powerless to institute genuine change in another person. So you can either accept or reject. That leaves you with only one loving option: to accept.

Putting Acceptance to the Test

One woman, for whom I have tremendous respect, found herself facing the most extreme test of acceptance versus approval. Helen had four children, but in only three did she take "pride and joy," as mothers say. Helen's prodigal daughter, Linda, had disappeared, then showed up on her doorstep one day as "Larry." Linda had undergone a sex-change operation. Taking heavy doses of male hormones, Linda was growing a mustache, and hair was sprouting on her chest.

Helen's shock and sorrow were inexpressible. "Larry" now wanted to rejoin the family as a son, and bring his partner with him. Helen knew that, whatever her decision was, the rest of the family would follow suit. After a period of mourning and adjustment, she decided she would either have to reject her daughter's new identity or swallow her pride and accept the poor choice exactly as it had been made.

Something supernatural began to happen in Helen as she humbled herself to accept "Larry." God gave her amazing grace. Because of her loving example, the family is wholly intact today, and Helen's decision has brought back that loving feeling. You may shake your head and say, "I could never do that; acceptance like *that* is beyond me." But I believe that kind of acceptance is possible for almost all of us.

I think about writer Corrie ten Boom's dear elderly Papa, who saw her worrying about the impending conflict in

Holland as Hitler's troops moved nearer. I heard Corrie tell that she was sure she couldn't face what was to come. Her papa gently reminded her, "Corrie, when you were little and Papa used to take you to the train, when did he hand you the ticket?"

"Just before I got on," she answered.

"And so will God," Papa wisely explained.

When your heart is right, God will give you what you need when you need it. Paul's letter to the Ephesians encourages us to accept and have patience: "Bearing with one another in love,... keep the unity of the Spirit in the bond of peace" (Eph 4:2-3). If God expects us to be accepting of others as our first step toward reconciliation, he will provide us with the ability to do so. As with Corrie ten Boom, he won't give us the grace we need until we need it. But it will be there. And as we learn to accept, we ready ourselves for the next step in loving our porcupine people. Once you've identified who they are, buckle your seat belt, for the ride of your life is about to begin! Against all odds you are going to love them, in spite of everything. If you absorb what you read, putting these ABCs into practice, you'll be pleased with the results! It's possible to love again. It all starts with acceptance.

Reflections

1. Give three reasons why you think every human being has value.
2. Is there someone you feel isn't living up to his or her potential? Does that opinion affect your relationship with this person?

3. What were you like when you were a new Christian? What did God have to overlook to love you?

4. Explain the difference between acceptance and approval.

5. How do the following help or hinder change in another person?
   - Prayer
   - Criticism
   - Acceptance
   - Encouragement
   - Unquestioning approval

6. What does the expression "tough love" mean to you?

SIX

B=Believe the Best!

I had just finished speaking to an enthusiastic group and was feeling elated by their response to my message on learning to love porcupine people. Then a woman approached me in tears. "Do you have just a minute?" she whispered.

"Of course," I said, taking her arm and guiding her toward a couple of nearby chairs. After such a receptive audience, my mind was racing to imagine what had brought her to tears. I asked, "Are you upset about something I said?"

"Well, not exactly. It's just that you got me started thinking about my brother...." Melissa's eyes flooded, and she sniffled into a tissue. "We've haven't talked for so long, and we used to be so close."

"What happened?"

"Well, he's had trouble with drugs. For a while he was stealing things to support his habit. Our family agreed it would be best to cut him off with no contact because we couldn't believe a word he said. We couldn't trust him. Today when you were talking about *believe* being a step toward reconciliation, I felt so sad, because if I have to believe him, I can never be close to him."

"So you want to be in touch, but you need to have some sense of control over him and his behavior?" I said.

Melissa nodded. "I want to be in touch, to be friends, to be able to laugh and talk on the phone the way we used to. But I can't let him into my home too freely, and I can't bring myself to believe he's trustworthy." She sighed and shook her head. "He just isn't."

As we talked, it occurred to me that learning to believe in situations like this involves important truths. These truths not only make reconciliation possible but provide some protection from further breaks in relationship. When we want to love again, what can we believe?

- We believe that God wants us to be reconciled with others, and helps us accomplish that goal.
- We believe in the goodness in others, focusing our attention on their strengths, not their weaknesses.
- We believe relationships are possible between imperfect people if clear boundaries are in place.
- We believe that love overcomes evil with good.
- We believe that God works all things together for good.

Believe in Reconciliation

Throughout Scripture, there is a clear call to unity among God's people. God is love. Refusal to love is against his nature and his will. Paul wrote, "Anyone united with the Messiah gets a fresh start, is created new. The old life is gone; a new life burgeons! All this comes from the God who settled the relationship between us and him, and then called us to settle our relationships with each other" (2 Cor 5:17-19 THE MESSAGE).

As we seek to bring back that loving feeling to relationships that are strained, we are acting out an aspect of Christian life that is important to God. We are ambassadors of Christ, demonstrating his forgiving love to others by not holding their faults against them. In reaching out to porcupine people, we are "putting skin on" God's efforts to reach them.

How does God show love for us? By forgiving our faults, overlooking our weaknesses, drawing us to himself and then, over the course of a lifetime, transforming us on the inside until we gradually become more like him. This doesn't mean that in the process God is fooled by our excuses, oblivious to our outbursts, or blind to our dishonesty. God certainly isn't in denial about us. In fact, his formula is, "You will know the truth, and the truth will set you free" (Jn 8:32 NIV). He simply chooses to love us, warts and all. And that's the way he wants us to love each other.

At the same time, there is every indication that one of the devil's favorite tactics is "divide and conquer." Satan wants to see us separated from God and separated from each other. I have an inspiring statue on my desk. Three monkeys remind me to see no evil, hear no evil, speak no evil. They are sitting next to a big stone, painted with these words: "The first stone." This reminds me of Jesus, who said, "He who is without sin ... let him be the first to throw a stone" (Jn 8:7 NASB). The monkeys remind me that I must refuse to believe the worst and cling to believing the best. It isn't that I choose to be unaware of other people's sins, flaws, weaknesses and bad habits. The point is that I choose to remember I have plenty of my own.

By choosing to love—in spite of—we are verifying *through our behavior* that we believe in love above all else. We are showing that people are more important than issues, and other people's weaknesses are less important than our own. When we love, we refuse to allow anything to interfere with our belief that love conquers all.

Keep the telephone of your mind open to love. Then whenever anger or criticism tries to call, they'll get a busy signal.

Believe in Others

An old adage asks, *when it comes to the person you are trying to love, where are you—in their balcony or in their basement?* Are you booing and heckling your porcupine person? Or are you cheering and applauding him or her? From time to time, every one of us has someone in our life who pulls us down. When these people compare their strengths to our weaknesses, we come up short.

They are negative and pessimistic, and the echo of their voices bounces off our walls:

- You'll never make it!
- It just won't work.
- If you had a brain you'd be dangerous.
- You'll never amount to anything.

- Don't get your hopes up.
- Who do you think you are?

I don't know about you, but I've had enough experience with that kind of audience to last a lifetime. And the last thing I want to do to another person is be that kind of a friend. Instead of throwing tomatoes, let's choose to throw bouquets! Everybody needs at least one person who will watch over his or her life from the balcony. From an elevated position we call others to go higher:

- You can make it!
- Go ahead and try anyhow!
- Failing doesn't make you a failure.
- You are unique and gifted.
- There is nothing you can't do if you keep trying.
- I believe in you!

Sometimes, encouraging other folks directs them to exhort and provoke *us* to good works. Dr. James Dobson expressed thanks to his wife for believing the best in him, by saying on their twenty-fifth wedding anniversary, "I still love the girl who believed in me before I believed in myself."[1] Wouldn't it be wonderful to provide that kind of support for your porcupine person? "Well," you're saying, "my _____" (spouse/friend/sister/brother/boss) "is no James Dobson!" So what? Give what you can give. Find something positive about him or her to brag about. Reach deeper within yourself for that tough love.

After attending one of my seminars, a young woman named Lori Gonzalez penned this:

Are you in my balcony or basement?
I asked my friend one day.
Sometimes I get confused, because of what you say.
You claim that you are teasing—
to get a laugh, you say.
But what you still don't understand,
is my heart takes it another way.
Our words can be a blessing
or a curse, and so,
Be careful what you say,
before you let it go.
Then one day you'll notice
there's a cheering from above.
Your own balcony is brimming
with the people that you love.
The words we say have power
to encourage or destroy.
Won't you stand in someone's balcony
and fill another life with joy?

Smart and pretty as Jennifer was, she was a shy teenager, and her parents worried about her shortage of friends. No matter how they tried to encourage her, she seemed reluctant to reach out socially. Then, her senior year, she started bringing home girlfriends after school and for weekend sleepovers. The girls would all go into Jennifer's bedroom and stay there. They'd come and go with barely a wave or a goodbye, as Jennifer's mother tried to reach out with friendly gestures that seemed in vain. Jennifer became more reclusive, too. Even the offer of yummy snacks didn't help lure the girls into the kitchen or den. They'd scarf down the pizza quickly, then retire to their privacy.

Now Jennifer had plenty of friends but started avoiding her family. What were her parents to do? Should they now forbid her to see friends? Should they compliment the new direction her life was taking? They felt helpless and confused. After talking about it together, they decided to find all the good they could in the situation and start affirming that in Jennifer. They told her they liked her girlfriends coming over and that her friends were always welcome in their home. They bought Jennifer a couple of new CDs they knew she wanted, so the girls could listen to them together. They started asking their daughter interesting and fun questions about her friends. They tried getting to know them through Jennifer's eyes first.

The "balcony" approach seemed to open a door. Jennifer became gradually less private and possessive of her friends at home. The girls would break for snacks more often, hang out longer in the kitchen, and tolerate Jennifer's father's "lame" jokes. Little by little, Jennifer and her family fused again. By graduation, the family threw a party for Jennifer and her friends. Grown-ups and kids ate, danced and played together at a backyard barbecue. Jennifer's parents had learned to lighten up, listen more, hang in there and be their daughter's biggest fan.

> **Y**ou can make a mountain out of a molehill or a molehill out of a mountain!

When is the right time to believe the best about somebody who has a poor track record? The sooner, the better! It has to happen before they deserve it, before they are worthy of it, if we are going to be conformed to Jesus' commandment to "love one another; as I have loved you" (Jn 13:34).

"Pray for a short memory to all unkindness," Charles Spurgeon wrote.[2] The Bible encourages us to begin practicing this pattern of thinking.

> Finally ... whatsoever things are true ... honest ... just ... pure ... lovely ... of good report; if there be any virtue ... any praise, think [dwell] on these things.
>
> PHILIPPIANS 4:8 KJV

Believe in Carefully Set Boundaries

There is another side to the issue of overlooking faults: protecting ourselves from further damage done by those who have hurt us. By keeping a short memory to unkindness, do we open the door to more heartache? In the next chapter, we will discuss the important (and difficult) subject of confrontation. But for now, let's look at one essential element of confrontation involving relationship rules, sometimes called "boundaries."

Cheryl, always a strong believer in Jesus, became a Roman Catholic when she got engaged to Jerry. They wanted to be able to take their future children to church together. But Cheryl's father was a Baptist deacon, who had always held a strong, even prejudicial dislike for the Roman Catholic church. He thought all Catholics were destined for hellfire and damnation and was always ready to remind Cheryl that she was in deep trouble, spiritually speaking. He felt commissioned by

God to share his opinion with his daughter.

Needless to say, Cheryl and her father became alienated from each other. When he walked in her house and saw the crucifix on the wall or one of his grandchildren wearing a "holy medal," he hit the roof. Cheryl's response was to avoid her father, refuse to go to his home or invite him to hers, and basically exclude him from her life.

Eventually, one of the grandchildren asked how his mother and grandfather could possibly love God and yet hate each others' churches. Cheryl and her father decided to work out some kind of a truce, agreeing their relationship was more valuable than endless debate. That truce involved boundaries: Cheryl would involve her father in her life again; her father would keep his opinions about the pope to himself. Neither denied the importance of their own point of view.

Different kinds of boundaries were necessary for Melissa, the woman we met earlier whose brother was struggling with drug addiction. She had to determine just what risks she was taking by letting her brother back into her life. She had to place limits on their relationship. Melissa made rules about giving her brother access to her house, for instance, because of the danger of theft. She chose to meet him in restaurants, where they could talk and laugh about their common interests. When he asked for money, she kindly told him she had none to spare, or if she did, she told him she wanted to keep money out of their relationship. When her brother's conversation strayed into inappropriate areas, Melissa gently changed the subject. It was awkward at first, but once the boundaries were in place, the friendship became more comfortable.

For Melissa, believing the best about her brother did not

mean pretending he didn't have a drug problem or thinking he could be treated like any other person she knew. It meant accepting him exactly as he was and forging a relationship around the danger zones his problems presented. In the future, Melissa may again have to suspend contact with her brother if drugs take over his life. But it won't be because she doesn't love him. Because of her efforts toward reconciliation, he knows that.

Believe That Good Overcomes Evil

Jesus had every reason to be discouraged at what he saw in the motley crew of twelve with whom he was supposed to leave the secrets of the kingdom. They didn't exactly seem to catch his drift. After crossing the Sea of Galilee in a boat, he warned them, "Beware of the leaven of the Pharisees" (Mk 8:15 KJV).

Peter quickly and confidently passed on his own interpretation to the rest: "I guess we forgot to bring the lunch." The disciples' lack of understanding went from bad to worse. The one to whom Jesus entrusted the treasury eventually sold his Lord for thirty pieces of silver. The one who loudly exclaimed he'd be the last person on earth to deny the Lord became the first to reject him. I imagine that Jesus had to adjust his thinking again and again. He might have prayed, "They sure don't seem like men who could ever be called *apostles*, Father, but there must be more to them than meets the eye. In any case, I trust in you. You've chosen them for me, so I'll just believe the best and carry on."

Even the miracle of the resurrection didn't resolve the

doubts or dysfunctions of the men who followed Jesus. Doubting Thomas couldn't see the reality of Jesus at all. *Hadn't Jesus died, after all?* he wondered. When Thomas' friends told him Jesus had risen from the dead, he replied, "unless I see … I will not believe" (Jn 20:25). For him, seeing was believing (was he from Missouri—the "Show Me" State— or what?)!

Jesus lovingly reprimanded Thomas,

"Blessed are those who have not seen and yet have believed."

JOHN 20:29

Jesus knew—and knows—that love overcomes evil. He allowed his disciples, his Jewish countrymen (and women), the Romans and everyone else involved to take his life. He knew that the resurrection power of love would bring him back to life and would transform the lives of all those who were touched by that power. He knows the same truth about us as modern-day disciples.

You may not see a reason to believe the best about your porcupine person, and you may be right! They may not even believe anything good about themselves yet. But by faith in the power of Christ to transform them (and us!), we can choose to see no evil, hear no evil, speak no evil. We don't do this because the evil is not there. We do it because, in spite of the presence of evil in the world, God has promised to bless those who, by faith, still believe in good!

> Treat people as if they were what they ought to be, and you help them to become what they are capable of being.

So much of our negative opinion of others has to do with our viewpoint. If you make a trip to the United Kingdom, you'll notice something that might make you chuckle. I laughed out loud when I saw a tow truck—we call them "wreckers"—on a British street with some interesting words painted on the side: "Recovery Vehicle." Mind you, these are the same trucks, with the same messy work to do. One bears a true but unflattering description. The other's mission is conveyed with words of grace.

Is there any harm in using positive, supportive words? Picture the proverbial proud mama, brimming with pride for her child who can do no wrong. She is constantly complimenting and building him up: "You are so bright. No wonder your teachers don't understand you—you're advanced! You need to be in a more accelerated class. Darling, you're going to be a doctor, a very important doctor." But too many of us are not like that. Our parental fear of causing swelled heads among our children does no one any favors. Most children get their swelled heads sufficiently deflated on the playground anyway, among their peers. Parents are their best source of reinflation and should relish the role as positive encouragers. That doesn't mean we don't point out important problems (more about that later). It means we balance any necessary criticism with plenty of wholehearted applause.

> Try to catch someone ...
> doing something GOOD!

Believe in God's Unseen Hand

When we view the world through the eyes of faith, everything changes shape. We view financial problems as reminders to look to God as our only source. We see a prodigal daughter or son as a beloved child of God, in the process of building a testimony for Christ. We see adversity as an opportunity to watch God's unseen hand work all things together for good. As Christians, most of us have learned that crummy circumstances are not something God delivers us *from* but something he will carry us *through*.

The apostle Paul admonishes, "Set your mind on things above" (Col 3:2). Believe that your circumstances with your porcupine person will be higher than where you are now—scrounging around, grappling with petty problems. Believe the best!

We do not look at the things which are SEEN, but at the things which are NOT seen.

2 CORINTHIANS 4:18

Reflections

1. Would you say you were in your porcupine person's *balcony* or *basement*? Do you think they sense your support? Do you cheer them on? Or would they say you never really believed in them?

2. Close your eyes for a moment, picturing your porcupine person. Can you see how God has blessed you in the past through him or her? Begin to see how that may be possible again. Picture him or her with genuine joy and contentment. See that person reaching out for you; trusting you again, sure you are endeavoring to believe the best about them.

3. Can you think of a time when you refused to believe something good about a person or a situation? What were the consequences?

4. Describe a difficult situation in your life. List five ways God could turn it into a blessing.

SEVEN

C=Confront With Care

Lana had been staying in her sister's guest room for more than three months and had long since worn out her welcome. Just like a porcupine, when she felt a threatening conversation approaching, her defensive quills would jut out. Iris had lost more than that loving feeling; even *liking* Lana was a strain.

One evening, Iris went into the guest room while Lana was out to look for a box of files in the closet. When she walked in, she caught her breath in dismay. The place was a disaster—clothes strewn everywhere, half-eaten food lying around, trash cans overflowing. It was one thing to have a human guest, but before long, rats and roaches might be moving in, too. When Iris talked about it with her husband, he always reacted the same way. He'd click the mute button on the remote, sigh, and say, "Just tell her to get out!" Then he'd shrug impatiently and ask, "Why are you making such a big deal out of it? It's really very simple."

But for Iris it wasn't simple at all. Lana's husband had died a year before; her children were away at college. Although

Lana's grief and loneliness were obvious, Iris resented her sister's thoughtlessness in staying, rent-free, for too long. Compassion prevented Iris from booting Lana out, while fear of confrontation held her back from addressing the problem.

But one night Iris woke up at four in the morning, tossing and turning, trying to resolve her frustration. She climbed out of bed, went down the stairs to the kitchen and poured herself a glass of milk. Enough was enough, she decided as she considered her options. She had already tried the silent treatment. She had hinted broadly. She had asked about Lana's travel plans on more than one occasion, and Lana's answer was always the same: "Who knows? I'm just playing things by ear right now."

Like a heavy weight, the truth was an enormous burden to Iris, but it was inescapable. She would have to confront her sister, explain that Lana had abused her privileges, and ask her to leave. Iris was nearly sickened by the thought of such a difficult conversation. She recalled many guilt trips for which she had signed on with Lana, who had a knack of making others feel responsible for her. In fact, Iris thought, *Lana is the East Coast distributor for guilt!*

Iris kept her weary vigil until the first light of a new day began to glow outside the kitchen window. *I'll do it tomorrow,* she promised. Then glancing at the clock, she shook her head sadly. *No,* she corrected herself. *I'll do it today. I'm starting to hate her, and I don't want that to happen. Better to get all this behind us.*

Confronting the Word *Confront*

Does the word *confrontation* make you feel uneasy? If so, you aren't alone. It pushes all kinds of emotional buttons on many people.

- "Oh, we had a little confrontation" is usually a nice way of saying that you've survived an extremely unpleasant conversation. (OK, so you had a knock-down-drag-out!)
- "Have you confronted him?" often means that you've heard a nasty little secret and know somebody needs to nail the guilty party.
- "I'm just going to have to confront this!" probably means that something has become so intolerable that you're willing to suffer the worst kind of emotional upheaval to resolve it.

Although there are people who rather enjoy "taking the bull by the horns" (as they cheerfully call it), most of us would rather experience *flight* than *fight,* and we therefore make it our habit to avoid confrontation at all costs. That doesn't mean we're right. It simply means that we choose to take the course of least resistance.

Taking the First Step

Like it or not, one of the essential elements in learning to love again is confrontation. But our goal is reconciliation rather than revenge. We determine not to *blow* up but to *show* up. We are advised in Scripture to speak the truth in *love*, not in anger or attack (see Eph 4:15). So we'll first have to pray that God will grant us the love we need in order to speak the truth. That doesn't sound so bad, does it? No, except for one thing: someone has to suggest the coming together. And if you're the one who wants to learn to love again, you may be the one who needs to take the first step.

Reconciliation is a two-way street, and unless both parties in a bruised, broken or battered relationship want to rebuild, reconciliation is impossible. The only way to get there at all is for one to confront the other, place his or her concerns on the table in love, and allow the other person to decide if she or he is willing to work together or not. That's the *bad* news for us nonconfrontational types. But there's also *good* news: confrontation doesn't have to mean fighting, arguing, scrapping, screaming or otherwise warring with one another. It simply means coming together, articulating the problem, and allowing the other person to choose whether to be part of the solution or not. If so, you both move toward a fresh start. If not, you move toward a fresh start alone.

Such a prospect may not be particularly appealing to you … or to your digestive system. If the idea causes a flock of butterflies to swarm up into your stomach, read on. You may learn that it isn't as scary as you think, because you can do certain things to make your meeting a positive experience. Confrontation is a big choice, but if it is to be effective it involves making many small and significant choices in the process.

You Choose the Right Time

Timing is everything. In his wonderful book *Dr. Roseberg's Do-It-Yourself Relationship Mender*, Dr. Gary Roseberg says, "Choose a time when you won't be hurried, when you can really communicate. Make it a time when you're both rested, when you won't have any outside distractions, and when your emotions will have cooled down."[1]

If the person you're dealing with is someone you know very well (like your sister or brother), you probably won't have to ask about the right time. But if you are dealing with a friend or a coworker who is not well known to you, you may wish to say,

- "When you've got time, I'd like to talk to you about something important to me."
- "There's something I want to talk over with you. When is a convenient time?"
- "Could you spare me a few minutes during lunch tomorrow, or is that a good time to talk?"
- "I know we haven't seen much of each other lately, but I miss you, and I'd really like to talk. Do you have any time today or tomorrow?"

Be sure you ask with a sincere smile and a friendly voice. Whatever you do, don't make it sound like you're going to teach the other person a lesson they won't soon forget. And remember, especially for husbands, "Can we talk?" can be the most terrifying three words in the English language. And we know what involuntary response that causes in porcupines! Be sensitive to the way he hears your request for communication. Try to take the threat out of it. Try, "Hey, Honey, I'd like to talk later. It won't take long. It's nothing earthshaking, but let's have coffee before bed, OK?"

You Choose the Right Place

Choose a location that is pleasant, private and, if possible, neutral territory to both of you. In the last chapter, we talked about Melissa, whose brother was a drug addict. She chose to confront him in a restaurant, where she also met him socially once her boundaries were in place. This gave her a sense of security about her home and didn't force him to invite her to his untidy apartment. They were both comfortable meeting on neutral turf.

Iris decided not to choose "neutral territory" for her meeting with Lana. Instead, she confronted her sister in the guest room first thing in the morning. Lana's mess was all around them as they talked, concrete evidence of trespassing upon openhearted hospitality. The disorder underscored Iris' words. Overwhelming evidence softened Lana's heart. Lana and Iris cried together and came to a mutual agreement on housekeeping and the appropriate time for Lana to move out.

Also, if you or the person you plan to meet has children, try to avoid having them present. The interruptions will raise everyone's blood pressure, and the issues will get lost in the process.

You Choose the Right Attitude

In *Caring Enough to Confront,* David Augsburger makes these astute suggestions:

- "Confront **caringly.** Only after experiencing real care for the other do you confront primarily to express real concern for another.
- "Confront **gently**. Do not offer more than the relationship can bear. Do not draw out more than you have put into the friendship.
- "Confront **constructively.** Take into consideration any possible interpretations of blaming, shaming, punishing.
- "Confront **acceptingly**. Respect the other's intentions as always good.
- "Confront **clearly**. Report what is fact (observation), what is feeling (emotion), what is hypothesis (conclusion)."[2]

Of course, the right reason to confront your porcupine person is that you deeply desire to rebuild the love you once had for him or her. But sometimes our motives are mixed. Most people feel empowered by anger and bitterness. And the thought of a good excuse to put the other person in his or her place may seem like a nearly irresistible temptation. That brings us to reasons *not* to confront:

- *Do not confront when you are still too angry to control yourself.* Take time to cool down.
- *Do not confront when it's none of your business.* You may have heard about a minor wrong that was done to your grown

children, your spouse or some friend of yours. Is it your place to meddle? In an instance of abuse it may be, but proceed with caution. Talk to the victim first.

When someone tries to share some juicy gossip with you, you have every reason to say, "I don't like what you're saying about my friend," but should you take on a confrontation about someone else's business? Probably not, especially if you'd relish the chance to set them straight.

- *Don't confront if you aren't sure about what happened.* Hearsay evidence is not acceptable in court. It shouldn't be grounds for a confrontation, either. If somebody told you that somebody told her that Suzy said something bad about you, don't go running to Suzy in a rage and try to teach her a lesson. Until you have strong evidence to believe you have been wronged, ask God to fight your battle for you and give him time. He is remarkably able to handle unjust situations and be your defense.

- *Don't confront when it's wise to overlook the offense.* There are some matters that are made worse by a confrontation. Suppose you are dealing with a difficult mother-in-law, and she makes a subtle, belittling statement about you. You hear her loud and clear. You get the message. You know, without the slightest question, exactly what she meant by what she said. But will confronting her make any difference? She probably isn't going to change her attitude or apologize if she's eighty years old. Chances are, she'll turn the whole thing around and humiliate you. She may have been hoping to get a reaction from you.

If someone "gets your goat," that only means you've got a

goat to get! And they can't get it if you don't tell them where you tied it.

Along similar lines, Jesus made this interesting statement: "Do not give what is holy to the dogs; nor cast your pearls before swine, lest they trample them under their feet, and then turn and tear you in pieces" (Mt. 7:6). Besides the fact that it can be dangerous to confront certain people, it can also simply be a waste of time. There are some individuals who are incapable of receiving words of love (these are the "pearls" they trample under their feet). In dealing with insensitive or intentionally unkind people, don't confront. It's likely a waste of time.

- *Do not confront when it's dangerous—physically, emotionally or spiritually.* It's always wise to avoid unpleasant scenes with violent people. The same is true of verbally or otherwise abusive people. Whoever said, "Sticks and stones can break my bones, but words can never hurt me" wasn't living in the real world.

You've now been given fair warning about what *not* to do. If you've determined that your porcupine person and your issues with him or her don't fit into the "don't confront" category, you'll need to prepare yourself for the occasion. How can you keep the conversation from igniting and turning into an inferno or freezing into an icicle? There are four things you can do to keep your confrontation on track.

1. Focus on the Issue.
It is easy for people with strong emotions to wander off the subject, fly off the handle or otherwise get diverted from the

focus of confrontation. Before you begin, it is wise to say something like: "The situation I want to discuss with you is ____. If I get off the subject, please get me back on track, and I'll try to do the same for you, so we can resolve this problem. Would that work for you?"

If for some reason this approach doesn't work, a quiet "Let's not get sidetracked; it's important for us to stick to the subject we're both concerned about" can help steer the subject back into focus.

2. Focus on "I," not "you."

When you address the incident, attitude or offense, don't start the conversation in an accusative way. Don't begin with the word *you*, saying, "You really made me mad!" or "You have this lousy habit of ..." or "How could you do that to me?"

Instead, start with the word *I*. Say, "I felt angry when you said ...," or "I feel frustrated by your habit of ...," or "I felt terribly hurt when you...." This removes the tone of accusation from the conversation, opening it up to a nondefensive response.

> Your intention isn't to win. It is to create an atmosphere where you both can learn how to communicate and rebuild your relationship.

PROPERTY OF
HIGH POINT PUBLIC LIBRARY
HIGH POINT, NORTH CAROLINA

3. Focus on Growth.

It may be difficult for you to accept the fact that you, too, have contributed to the problem you're having with your porcupine person. There is, in fact, usually an equal amount of blame on both sides. If you approach the confrontation with a plan to apologize for the part you've played in the problem, you will be on your way toward personal growth—emotional and spiritual—and growth in your relationship.

If you enter into your confrontation with a willingness to hear the other person out, admit your faults, learn from your mistakes and make amends, you'll have traveled a long way toward resolving the issues. But more important, demonstrating your humility and vulnerability will enable the other person to believe that it's possible to rebuild the relationship.

If your porcupine person accuses you of something you don't feel you've done, what do you do? Take time out. Instead of reacting defensively, say, "Well, I'll have to think about that. I haven't looked at it that way before." Then move on with the conversation. Remember, you didn't seek the confrontation in order to defend yourself. You are simply seeking a new beginning, and not every point of argument has to be settled. Sometimes we simply have to agree to disagree.

4. Focus on Gentleness and Mutual Understanding.

Paul wrote, "Let your gentleness be evident to all. The Lord is near" (Phil 4:5 NIV). Does gentleness mean being wimpy or weak? No. It means that you are putting love ahead of everything else. In other words, the person you're talking to is more important than the issue you're talking about. A spirit of gentleness leads us into a desire to understand.

Once we've set aside our need to win the argument, to come out on top, to get the last word, we can begin to concentrate on the other person's point of view. Why did she act that way? What was going on in his mind? What makes your porcupine person tick? We certainly don't have to understand the other person to forgive, but understanding helps us a great deal when we are trying to reconcile a damaged friendship. Confrontation can be a positive learning experience for both parties. It is meant to be an opportunity to gain understanding.

Confronting an Alcoholic

After dating for a couple of years, Kathleen found it necessary to confront her boyfriend about his drinking. For several months, she'd been concerned about Jason's use of alcohol. It seemed to her that he was becoming more and more dependent on it. She was also beginning to notice an ugly flicker in Jason's eyes once he had a few drinks under his belt. Struggling with this, Kathleen's emotions swung from anger to fear to sadness. Sometimes she was furious at Jason for putting their relationship at risk. Sometimes she was afraid she would lose him if she raised the subject. She genuinely loved Jason. Their relationship had so much good in it. Sometimes she simply cried, wondering, *Why can't it be easier?*

As she wrestled with her ambivalence, Kathleen noticed she felt most like confronting Jason when she was angry. Rage seemed to overwhelm her fears, fuel her with courage and provide a confident tone of voice she couldn't seem to muster otherwise. But as a Christian, Kathleen detected an inner warning about keeping her cool. "Be gentle with him," she seemed to hear.

One day over lunch, after Jason had ordered his drink, Kathleen quietly said, "Jason, I'm worried about your drinking. I love you, and I'm concerned about both your emotional and your physical health. Can we talk about it a little?" Her gentle voice prevented Jason from feeling defensive. He admitted that he, too, had been aware of his increasing dependence on alcohol. "I've just got so much stress right now," he explained, "and I guess a few drinks make me feel less uptight. But that doesn't make it right. I know that."

Later, Jason agreed to participate in an alcoholic recovery group at Kathleen's church. His struggle didn't end overnight, but he got a handle on alcohol abuse before a crisis occurred. On more than one occasion he thanked Kathleen for confronting him in the right place, at the right time and in a quiet way. "If you'd lost your temper with me when I'd already been drinking, I would have lost my temper, too, and who knows what might have happened?" he said. "I'm so glad you loved me enough to confront me. But I'm even more glad you handled it with love."

Unfortunately, dealing with difficult people in love and understanding is no guarantee that all will be well. But if you choose to take this higher road, it will free you to know that you have done right. On a flight recently, the man two rows behind me was obnoxious. Everyone within five rows of this man was being disturbed by his loud voice and vulgar language. Like many others I needed to work in-flight; we all winced at the sound of his voice. I decided to bite the bullet. "Excuse me, sir," I said as I sheepishly approached him. "You're probably not aware of how your voice carries, and those around you would appreciate it if you could keep your voice down. Would you mind?"

"Are you a flight attendant?" he snapped back at me.

"No," I said, "just a fellow passen-"

"Then mind your own X@O#! business and sit down."

I felt the blood rushing to my head. I knew it showed. I put my emotional tail between my legs and limped back to my seat. The man across the aisle from me winked and gave me a thumbs-up. The flight attendant whispered, "Nice try!" as she slipped me another dessert!

Writing a Love Letter to a Porcupine

If it is impossible for you to arrange a face-to-face meeting in order to confront, a letter may be a good substitute. Authors John Nieder and Thomas Thompson suggest that a great deal of time be taken in writing such a letter. It should clearly communicate love and concern for the other person, seeking his or her forgiveness for whatever wrongs you may have done: "Never send a letter in haste. Ponder over it. Sleep on it. Be sure it says what you want it to say, reflecting your kind and gentle spirit, yet speaking the truth. Writing forces you to examine your thoughts. When you see your words on paper, they sometimes jump back at you. You may realize, *Maybe I'm to blame. Maybe I'm at fault at least as much as he is.* You may even decide that a confrontation is not necessary. Writing will help you place a healthy distance between your words and your emotions. An unpleasant flare-up may be avoided."[3]

If a person who has offended you has died before the issue was confronted, a letter may still be a helpful tool in resolving your anger and laying the matter to rest. Putting your thoughts on paper can give you a sense of closure and will provide an opportunity for you to work through the issues, even though you can no longer talk to that loved one.

Confrontation Is a New Beginning

As we continue to work through the ABCs of learning to love again, each requires hard work, humility and hope. In each case, rewards far outweigh the challenges. Confrontation remains one of the most difficult, yet necessary, steps toward rebuilding relationships. If it seems impossible to you right now, please don't stop reading and give up on the whole idea of reconciliation with your porcupine person. Instead, leave the subject for now and turn to the chapters that follow.

While you are reading, ask God to show you what he'd like you to do. If confrontation isn't necessary or wise, he'll let you know. If it is part of his plan, he'll guide you, giving you wisdom and strength to meet the challenge. You can be sure that if it's something God wants, he will bless your efforts, work out the details and strengthen you in the process.

Care enough to confront.

Reflections

1. Ask yourself, why do I need to confront my porcupine person? Is it because of:
   - an incident?
   - an attitude?
   - a statement?
   - an impasse?
   - a behavior pattern?
   - a misunderstanding?
   - a betrayal?
   - a lie?
   - a disappointment?

   Getting focused will enable you to pinpoint hurt and avoid generalities when you confront this person, who may already have his or her quills standing straight up.

2. What emotions does the word *confrontation* stir up inside you? Describe your feelings.

3. Have you ever had a confrontation that turned out for the best? Write your thoughts about it, including what you said and why you believe it worked out well.

4. Why do you think anger is such a tempting tool to use in a confrontation? Journal your ideas about the pros and cons of speaking the truth in anger.

5. Write a confrontational letter to your porcupine person. After you've finished, put it away for a few weeks and ask God to guide you about whether to send it or not.

6. Evaluate your letter based on the focus issues from this chapter.

7. Practice expressing your feelings on paper before you have to confront. In order to prepare your heart and mind, express who you are, what you think, what you feel and what your needs are.

EIGHT

D=Decide to Improve Your Relationship

My dear friend Clyde is what I would call a VRW, a Veteran of Religious Wars. He has survived more than his share of disappointments in the church, and many a preacher has taken advantage of his financial success. Consequently, Clyde is wounded.

Some years ago, he decided no longer to be involved with any church, and, as time passed, the things of God became vague in his memory. Then one day, as Clyde concentrated on his land development business, he unexpectedly encountered God again. At the time, Clyde was sitting slumped over the steering wheel of his Mercedes, peering out over an old, dilapidated mobile home park. *How could I have possibly agreed to buy this piece of trash?* he wondered. Clyde felt deceived and betrayed by his real estate broker and even angrier with himself for not checking things out more thoroughly.

With a heavy heart, Clyde watched a ragged parade of human wreckage moving around the rusted Airstream trailers. There were bikers, old tattooed reprobates and loud-mouthed mothers screaming at filthy kids. Drug deals were even being negotiated right before his eyes! Clyde had never had any particular love for riffraff. The "low-lifers" were not his kind of people.

Clyde thought, *This is one investment I'll dump ASAP!* Then, a conflicting thought diverted his attention unexpectedly, startling him by the unmistakable words: "These are my people."

"God," he thought, "this is a total mess!"

"Right, and these are my people," persisted the voice.

It had been a long time since Clyde had heard from God. Tears began to well up in his eyes and drop onto the dashboard. Why would God refer to these pitiful people as *his?*

Clyde began putting things together. He understood that he had been fooled into buying this property for God's purposes—to help God's "people." He began to feel a familiar, warm stirring in his heart. Excited and inspired, he drove home, changed into jeans and then returned to the wreckage of the park in his old pickup. He hesitated to get out at first; the place didn't look like it welcomed strangers. Then he stepped boldly toward the first trailer and knocked on the door. When it opened he was struck by the sight and the smell. A grumpy elderly woman growled, "What the #&#@ do you want?"

Clyde spoke shyly: "I'm the new owner of this trailer park, and I wonder what I can do for you."

"I said, what do you want?"

"I want to help in some way. What do you think the park needs most?"

The woman laughed bitterly. "You might want to start by getting rid of the drug dealers and hookers." Her eyes narrow and suspicious, she continued, "But why would you care?"

Clyde swallowed hard and quietly explained, "Because God told me you are one of his people."

"What are you? Some kind of a Jehovah's Witness?"

"No, no."

"Are you a preacher then?"

"No, I'm just another one of God's people, and I think he's sent me to help." In that split second, Clyde realized he had decided to love these folks, lock, stock and barrel, come what may.

"Well, don't stand there in the heat," the woman muttered. "Come on in." That first knock opened up more than one door in that trailer park. But above all else, it opened Clyde's life to the moving of the Holy Spirit.

In the days and weeks that followed, the drug dealers and prostitutes were cleaned out. In fact, a few were even cleaned up! A young single mom told Clyde, "I'm afraid to send my kids outside. This ain't a street, it's a mud hole—and it's too dark at night, too." In response, Clyde was soon leading his work crew into the park, grading the streets, adding security lights, a washer and dryer, fencing the place—and even planting flowers! Gradually, a transformation took place. And not just with the trailer park. Clyde began to change, too, as he learned to love these folks.

Many of the residents began to take Clyde at his word. *Maybe God really did care.* Eventually, since the needs within each trailer home were so great, Clyde gave a trailer to a retired couple and asked them to be the "park missionaries," looking after the needs of God's beautiful people in the park!

Decide to Love the Unlovable

Because God decided to love us, we are able love one another, as Clyde did the residents of the trailer park. But the process gets blocked if we don't accept the fact that God loved us before we were the least bit lovable.

Do you feel loved by God? Perhaps you and God are like the couple driving down the highway. The husband is driving, and the wife, sitting as close as she can get to the passenger door, barks out, "What ever happened to us, Harvey? When we was first married and went for a drive, we sat so close, a body couldn't tell there were two people in the front seat!"

The husband quietly answered, "Well, dear, I never moved."

God is still in the driver's seat ... where he's always been. He is stationary, in his unchanging position. It is you and I who move away. Until we restore our relationship with him, we will have a difficult time learning to love anybody else.

God may be waiting to do something wonderful through you, to enable you to grow the beautiful fruit of the Spirit, which is love. But he needs you to get your hands dirty. Consider the story of an outstanding fruit and vegetable farmer in Oklahoma, well known for growing award-winning crops. A tourist visited his farm, viewed his produce and commented, "Look at the size of those zucchini, praise the Lord! I can't believe the size of those watermelons! Hallelujah! Thanks be to God, will you look at that crop of corn?"

The farmer listened for awhile, then commented, "Glad you're giving God the glory for the crop, son. But you should have seen this farm when God had it all by himself—there wasn't a thing that growed here!"

Learning to love again is a decision based on God's love for us and on our willingness to get our hands dirty and let him do his loving work through us.

> **W**e cannot do what God must do and God will not do what we must do!

Decide Not to Take Offense

When dealing with porcupine people, we are continuously tempted to be offended by them. For the sake of reconciliation, we have to make a new decision in that area: we must decide not to take offense at everything. As they reach out to hand us some outrage or other, we simply choose not to receive it.

Recently one of my relatives wrote me a nasty note, scolding me for being so distant. Because I didn't keep in closer touch by calling more often, he assumed I was becoming a hotshot. "Now that you're a big public speaker, I guess you're too important to care about us peons in the family."

Ouch! I could really take offense at that one! But instead I decided to lay it down, not pick it up. One part of me said, "Forget it. You can't please this person; he is bitter and jealous." Another part of me (the part that is closer to Christ) reminded me of the disappointing life this man now led and how deserted he must feel. Instead of choosing to ignore the letter, I decided to call and take my licks. This relative let me know in no uncertain terms that sending a postcard from some distant city in which I was speaking made him feel more distant than ever. He wasted no words. Finally, after being soundly taken to task, I apologized.

Somehow, I was able to see how he could interpret my silence as meaning I didn't care about him anymore. I explained to him how hectic my schedule sometimes gets with writing, traveling and speaking. I said I wouldn't send any more postcards from far off places to irritate him. I assured him I did think of him even though we'd lost touch and pledged to try and do better in the future. By the time our phone conversation was over, he had cooled down and I felt connected rather than alienated from him.

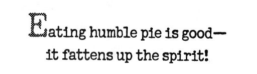

Eating humble pie is good—
it fattens up the spirit!

I've come to accept the fact that love is not like lightning: it doesn't strike suddenly, unannounced and unexpectedly. Opportunities to love may arise suddenly, as they did with Clyde, but our response requires a decision. The body of Christ is made for the building up of itself in love (see Eph

4:16), writes Paul. An attitude of love is more powerful than past experience. It overrides education, overshadows financial needs, overwhelms circumstances and overrules whatever other people may think. A loving attitude can make or break us. How great to know that every day we're given another chance to change our ugly, twisted, negative thinking and replace it with loving thoughts!

> **I**f you are headed in the wrong direction, God allows U-turns!

Decide to Love, No Matter How You Feel

I have a friend who struggles to parent a difficult teenage daughter. A (generous) bystander might say that the girl struggles with depression. A less generous person might describe her as being "attitudinally challenged."

One morning, the girl came downstairs for breakfast looking down in the mouth; a dark cloud was rapidly forming above her head. Her upbeat mom made a helpful suggestion: "Honey, I'll bet if you put a little smile on your face today, something good might happen!"

The daughter sarcastically replied, "If I acted happy, it would be phony!"

"Trust me," said Mom, "phony happiness is better than genuine depression!"

Hannah Hurnard put it another way in her classic book,

Mountains of Spices. She was struggling to love a fellow worker with whom she shared a mutually antagonistic relationship. Deciding to love again, she made the decision to act lovingly, whether she *felt* it or not. Later, she wrote, "It is better to go stumbling and weeping, and crawling along the way of love than to give up. For desiring to love a person, and trying to act lovingly at a time when we do not feel love is in actual fact crawling along the way of Love. For it is never hypocrisy to act as we earnestly desire to feel."[1]

Decide to Be Committed

There is a world of difference between merely being involved with a person and being committed to him or her. It is as different as ham and eggs. When it comes to breakfast, the chicken is involved, but the pig is totally committed!

In today's self-centered society, we seem to have relegated the idea of commitment to the archives. Few people seem to understand what it means to make a solid commitment, to obligate ourselves to do our duty. In churches, people "commit" to attend a Bible study. The night rolls around and the hostess puts out the cookies, but no one shows up. In marriages, the commitment to remain married "for better or for worse" means nothing. If staying with a spouse doesn't feel good, many back away.

My friend was counseling a man who told him, "I need more space. If I stay married, with three kids, I can't be all that I can be."

The counselor replied, "If you want to be all that you can be, join the army! Marriage is not about self-realization, it's about laying down your life."

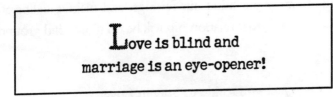

Love is blind and marriage is an eye-opener!

Somebody asks, "Did you ever fall in love?"

"No," his friend answers, "but I have stepped in it a few times."

When I was young, I thought we had little control over this "love" thing. So I fell in love with my husband, Hal, one day. It seemed to me that love was similar to a beautiful, white dove, descending toward us. I believed that when it suddenly landed on our shoulder (without our being aware), a feeling of love would spread throughout our being.

Then one day that miserable bird messed all the way down my back!

Believe me, I didn't feel "in love" anymore. But I decided to stay. Why? Because ...

Committing to love involves making a willful decision, followed by loving behavior, which produces loving feelings.

It's important to clarify something here: although some may have fallen into love, none of us have ever fallen into commitment. Commitment requires a willful decision. In fact, if we temporarily put aside our feelings, and make a deliberate *decision* to love, that relationship will be on more solid ground.

Decide to Stay in Love

A friend of mine put it this way: "I married my wife, Nancy, because I loved her. Now I love Nancy because I married her." How wise.

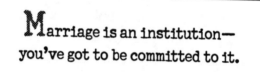

Marriage is an institution—
you've got to be committed to it.

We are willing to commit ourselves to a job, a church, our kids, even to our automobiles! We give whatever our car needs in order to keep it running smoothly. We check the oil, top off the gas and fork over money for maintenance and insurance. We gauge the tires, wash the outside, vacuum the inside and do our best to keep our vehicle in reasonably good condition. Seems to me, it should be at least of equal importance to treat a spouse as well as we'd treat a car—in fact, the last car we'll ever own!

"But Lee, you don't understand," you say. "I just don't feel anything for my husband anymore. The love in me is dead. Finished. Kaput!"

Believe me, I've heard that one a few times. And thank God, the relationship is not over when the feelings are gone. It may just need a major overhaul.

To be candid, I'd have to say that I've gone through that kind of emotional wasteland myself. In all the years Hal and I have been married and have raised children together, I've had all kinds of feelings—from red-hot romance to stone-cold indifference. I've probably said it all over the years (at least I've thought it all):

- "I don't love you anymore—I don't even like you!"
- "We're just staying together for the kids' sake."
- "You leave me cold."
- "I can't believe I ever thought I was in love with you!"

However, now that I'm more than twenty years on the other side of marital ups and downs, I'm glad my commitment held steady! My husband and I have fought and struggled our way to a most satisfying, nourishing and healthy relationship. I can truthfully say that I wouldn't trade Hal for anyone now. (Richard Gere, eat your heart out!)

Decide to "Let" Love Happen

One of the Bible's most powerful and often-used words is a little three-letter one: *let*. The apostle John encourages us, "Let us love one another" (1 Jn 4:7). This involves a decision, a choice, a commitment. The word *let* can also be translated as "allow," "permit," "consent" or "yield to." Your cooperation is vital in deciding to become a more loving person. Will you be committed to love? Will you let love come? Will you commit yourself to love?

Here's what the Bible has to say about that:

- "Let us love one another, for love is of God" (1 Jn 4:7).
- "Let brotherly love continue" (Heb 13:1).
- "Let the peace of God rule in your hearts" (Col 3:15).
- "Let this [loving] mind be in you" (Phil 2:5).
- "Let love be without hypocrisy" (Rom 12:9).
- "Let us not love in word ... but in deed and in truth" (1 Jn 4:7).

I have made a commitment to God as a speaker: I have pledged to let love abound toward each audience to whom I speak. I know I must genuinely care about those who hear me, or I'll simply come across as a cold, distant "celebrity" from California doing another "gig." I'm convinced an unloving attitude quickly comes across to audiences. Come to think of it, I've suffered through some pretty hard-nosed lectures in churches myself.

But although I've made the commitment to love, it doesn't automatically happen each time I face a new crowd. Not every audience is warm and receptive; some are so dead you start to look for indications that they are breathing. Quite often, by the time I sit through all the hassles of getting to the event and wade through the preliminaries before I speak (including board meetings, lengthy song services, 103 announcements), I don't exactly feel love overwhelm me as I step up to the lectern.

I've devised a little system to remind myself of my commitment to love (I'm telling my secrets now). If you were to see my messy speaking notes, you'd chuckle; in addition to all the sprawled writing, shorthand and sticky notes, I've placed little red heart stickers periodically through my notes to ask myself, *Are you just lecturing, Lee? Just passing on information? Do these people matter to you? Look at their faces. Feel their need. Above all else, love them.*

Decide to See Through Eyes of Love

One Sunday I sat in yet another church service, bored again. *This guy is no prize,* I mused as I flipped through my Bible. His volume was set on "loud." He'd shock us periodically by punctuating his remarks with a resounding "Glory to God!" I remembered a time when I had actually enjoyed his messages, but, in my opinion, his sermon that day seemed absurdly shallow.

Fortunately, this was the point at which I was challenged to make a decision. Would I allow my boredom to be apparent, spreading it around with the other dissatisfied members after the service? Or would I choose the way of love? Could I learn to love this not-very-experienced young pastor again?

I began to pray something like this: "Lord, you have a firecracker on your hands with this guy! I thank you for his passion for the lost and his intensity of faith. As you see him,

Lord, I bet you smile. Yes, he has a lot to learn, but you can teach him through the instruction of those who love him. I pray for you to supply him with peers who will direct him into your ways and steer him out of bad preaching habits. Give him a mentor, someone who can help him in the maturing process."

By choosing love, I was also hoping God would enable me to kill off the critical and judgmental attitude I was fostering. It worked. Once I made this decision, even during his loud preaching, I could see him in a different light and thank God for his sincerity. Afterward I could genuinely remark, "You know, he honestly challenged me with his fiery spirit for God."

Anyone, then, who knows the good he ought to do and doesn't do it, sins.

JAMES 4:17 NIV

The Sacrifice of Love

This might be a good time to review the familiar "owe no man anything" passage (see Rom 13:8). Here's how it sounds translated so well in *The Message*:

Don't run up debts, except for the huge debt of love you owe each other. When you love others, you complete what the law has been after all along.... Love other people as well as you do yourself. You can't go wrong when you love others. When you add up everything in the law code, the sum total is *love!*

ROMANS 13: 7, 8 THE MESSAGE

The people whom God loves do not always appear to be the most desirable or best behaved. God's beautiful people are often in need of a good set of teeth, a more tasteful wardrobe or even a bath! God's people are often in need of better manners, good tempers, improved morale. When we learn the lessons of love it becomes easier to smile at people with dirty hair, to delight in the company of an attitudinally challenged person or to hug a person with bad breath and a big ego. God's Word reminds us that "not many wise, not many mighty, not many noble are called …"(1 Cor 1:26). We are to love anyway. How else might we unwittingly entertain angels (see Heb 13:2)?

Reflections

1. In romantic relationships, if you "fell" in love, by now you realize that "fallout" was all too easy. Decide right now to offer up this prayer: "I will love _____ with my mind, my will and my spirit. Lord, I'll let you worry about my emotions."

2. Renew—again—your unconditional commitment to love your porcupine person.

3. Picture that person with all his or her imperfections, then speak these words aloud as if he or she were there: "I am

making a decision to love you, imperfections and all. With God's help, I will see you through eyes of love."

4. Think of three recent examples where you had the opportunity to decide whether to take offense at another person's words or actions. What did you decide? Was your decision the loving one?

NINE

E=Effort Means Hard Work

While praying and seeking guidance for upcoming sermons, the pastor of one large church felt led to begin a series on the topic of love. The Lord spoke to his spirit immediately, saying, "Don't bother; you've preached on love many, many times, and they still don't get it."

Surprised, the pastor had to admit that was all too true. His parishioners did little more than attend services and go home. They managed to avoid getting close to each other for any reason.

When Sunday morning arrived, the minister sat on the platform, surveying his congregation. Once the choir had finished, he boldly stepped to the pulpit and declared, "The Bible says, 'Love one another!'" Having said that, he simply returned to his seat and sat down.

The congregation looked a little confused. They glanced at each other uneasily. Maybe a solo or an announcement was coming. After a few minutes of rustling and clearing of throats, the man stood once more in the pulpit and proclaimed, "The Lord Jesus commanded us, 'Love one another!'" Again he sat down. By this time, the crowd was getting restless, looking around for a cue.

The third time the admonition was repeated, a gentleman in the second row got the picture. He reached over and extended his hand to the couple seated on his right. He introduced himself, and they quietly began to chat, finding out that they lived not far from each other.

"Do you have any requests for prayer?" the gentleman inquired.

The couple shyly looked at each other. "Well," the husband sheepishly answered, "as a matter of fact, we do. I've been out of work for four months now. I really need a job."

"What do you do?"

"I am a carpenter. I do finish work," the man replied.

"I have an idea!" the first gentleman exclaimed. He signaled to a friend four rows behind them, a contractor, who had a big construction site going downtown.

Right then, on the spot, the contractor offered the unemployed man a job. "Just be there at seven in the morning," he told him.

The carpenter, his wife and the contractor rejoiced together that morning. A collection was taken for the needy couple. All over the church, similar incidents were taking place. For the first time, the congregation was learning the practical effort involved in loving one another. Before long, a revival broke out in the community.

"You can develop a healthy robust community that lives right with God and enjoy its results *only* if you do the hard work of getting along with each other, treating each other with dignity and honor."

JAMES 3:17 THE MESSAGE

Doing the Difficult Thing

Bringing back that loving feeling in to a porcupine situation is a process, not an event. As we've already learned in earlier chapters, our decision to love again doesn't provide immediate results. One of the important, long-term requirements for success is the E-word: Effort. This involves giving of ourselves on a continual basis in areas such as understanding, vulnerability, communication, loving actions and prayer. Like it or not, we're going to have to be totally involved and committed to the practice of love.

Some of us are a little like the husband who (finally) agreed to go to a marriage counselor with his wife. The poor woman was so nervous that as soon as she sat down, she began sniffling. Soon her tears turned into heavy weeping, and before long she seemed inconsolable. The husband remained seated, unmoved by her tears. The counselor got out of his chair and walked around the desk to embrace the woman. As he comforted her, the flood of tears subsided. Before long, she had composed herself.

The counselor turned to the husband and said, "Now, can you see what she needs?"

"Yeah, sure," replied the still-irritated husband, "I'll bring her here once a week!"

I hope that by now we are a step or two ahead of this rather confused man. We know very well that no one can take steps toward loving again *for us;* we'll have to make the effort ourselves. To begin with, we'll need to determine just what kind of effort is necessary, just what is needed.

Make the Effort to Understand

Do you understand what lies behind your porcupine person's not-so-appropriate behavior? It's easy to disapprove. It's easy to get hurt. It's not easy to step back and look at the situation from a different point of view. But this can be helpful, even if the person has already died.

For years, I struggled to come to terms with my abusive father's behavior during my childhood. He was an alcoholic and died young of cirrhosis of the liver; I retained enormous reservoirs of unresolved anger and unanswered questions as I grew. He was a violent man, staying most of the time in the basement of our home where he had crudely wallpapered the basement walls with pornographic pictures. Often he would emerge, ascending the stairs in fits fueled by alcohol.

For a long time, I could still remember the smack of the brutal cat-o'-nine-tails he had fashioned to punish us children. And even in his sober moments he disliked talking about anything personal, avoiding intimate conversations at any cost. Although I desired to love my father as an adult daughter, I felt powerless to conjure up positive thoughts about him.

After he died, in my quest to develop loving feelings for him, I began to look for redeeming factors and some explanation of his intolerable behavior. I was thirty-five years old before I got the answers I needed, stumbling across some background information that was enlightening and helpful. I was never told that my father was abandoned as a child, raised by reluctant relatives who changed his name, resulting in a haunting feeling of rejection. At this point of discovery I realized I had a choice. I could either keep my justified resentment toward my dad and dismiss the new information as "no excuse for putting his children through hell." Or I could factor it into the picture. Because I knew it was God's will that I choose to love, I picked the higher path. In making this effort, love and understanding for my deceased dad began to grow. I found myself regretting that I hadn't known more about him while he was still alive. It might have made a difference.

Today when I think of my father as *Daddy*, I don't get the old stabbing pain of resentment. I am less aware of the pain of abandonment and loss. Instead, I feel a sense of warmth, realizing that he was a broken man, emotionally deformed and crippled by life's injustices, who was merely doing the best he could.

I know firsthand that the effort toward understanding can provide a different point of view toward your porcupine person. It will not (and should not) excuse bad behavior, but it may restrain yours! Understanding, time and the ABCs in action may soften the person you are seeking to love. Might there be extenuating circumstances behind his or her offensive actions? Perhaps your attitude toward the person needs to communicate the following truth.

> Someone else has broken something in you. Now is your time to find the break and fix it.

So often, in an effort to protect ourselves from further injury, we put up defenses intended to keep emotionally dangerous people at arm's length. Sometimes that is appropriate when we are setting up our boundaries in a relationship. But you don't have to be a rocket scientist to know that loving requires vulnerability. The time will come when you will want to take off your emotional suit of armor.

On one particular occasion, I desperately wanted to protect myself from what I expected to be a hostile audience. When a group of feminists asked me to be a plenary speaker at a large convention that included speakers such as Lily Tomlin, Joan Rivers and Anita Hill, I was in shock. Why did they want me? I could only imagine that the humor I use when speaking must have opened the door. But because of our different views about much of life (and their reputation for loudly rejecting those who disagree), I began to build a defensive wall around myself. In order to protect myself, I bolstered my rejection of their way of life.

Gradually, however, God showed me that he could not use me in this difficult speaking arena unless I made the effort to view the women who would attend through nondefensive eyes. In order for the love of God to flow through me, I'd have to change my outlook (particularly when facing the large block of gay attendees). So I began to see them not as hard-core New Age women who reject all Judeo-Christian values but as disappointed women searching for answers.

I walked myself through this exercise of faith before I went to the convention, honestly seeking to feel compassion for them. I was genuinely surprised by the grace I found! My heart was so soft toward them, that rather than being repulsed I could almost feel their pain and disillusionment. Without compromise, I gave them my own version of what hope is all about and encouraged them to look to Christ. I did this not by preaching down to them but by feeling their anguish and offering godly answers. God uniquely blessed my sessions by opening the hearts of the listeners, and some precious seed was sown for his kingdom. One well-dressed professional came to me after a session. Her white blouse was stained with her mascara. "Thanks for reminding me about Jesus," she blurted out, "I honestly *forgot* about Jesus!"

> My little children, let us not love in word or in tongue, but in deed and in truth.
>
> 1 JOHN 3:18

Make the Effort to Communicate

Sometimes, after we have confronted a difficult individual with the issues that come between us, we think the job is done. We imagine that we are now able to carry on the relationship with no further problems. Unfortunately, this is rarely the case, and further communication is necessary if the friendship is to be fully restored.

Kelly had a grandson who was, in her humble opinion, the most beautiful, wonderful and brilliant one-year-old in the entire world. She bought him presents, showed his pictures to everyone who would look and told his antics to her friends again and again.

Needless to say, there was never a time when Kelly wasn't delighted to see little Travis. His big smile and warm hugs cheered her up, no matter what else was on her mind. But over a period of months, Kelly noticed that her daughter-in-law Sandi was dropping Travis off at her house more frequently. Sandi's reasons for leaving him were becoming rather lame. Kelly wondered why Sandi wouldn't take Travis to the market. He loved riding in the shopping cart, looking at all the colorful boxes and bottles and jars. He was always good, so there was no danger of his having a tantrum and terrorizing the other shoppers. When Kelly analyzed her feelings, she realized that she didn't mind watching Travis—that wasn't the point—it was the presumptuous way Sandi was behaving that finally forced her to speak up.

"Sandi, I know you're busy, but you seem to be leaving Travis here almost every day!" Kelly said.

Sandi sized her mother-in-law up coolly. "I thought you enjoyed him, Mom."

"Of course I enjoy him, Sandi. He's the light of my life. But you need to give me a little more warning. Yesterday and today, you didn't even call before you came."

"Well, I just figured I'd take him with me if you weren't here. So what's the problem?"

Kelly sighed and offered up a quick prayer. "You're right. I'm usually home. But I have a lot of things to do around here, and I have a sort of schedule for each day. When I get interrupted, I feel kind of frustrated because things don't get done."

"Like what?" Sandi looked genuinely surprised to hear that Kelly had a life beyond Travis' arrivals and departures.

"Well, I guess what I'm doing really isn't the point, Sandi." Kelly tried to smile a little. "What I'm saying is, let's plan ahead. Give me a couple of days' warning, and I'll be glad to have Travis while you're out. But I don't want to feel upset when you drive up unannounced. I love you both too much to let that happen."

Kelly's words stung Sandi, and she left the house rather abruptly. But after she had thought things over, she realized that she'd been taking advantage of Kelly's generosity. Within a week, she apologized, and from that point on, the two women were able to communicate clearly and honestly about Travis' visits.

Communication involves more than confronting or even reconfronting difficulties. It requires care in every aspect of every conversation when people aren't getting along. Consider these practical communication tips:

1. Think before you speak.
2. Choose your words carefully.
3. Ask for feedback: make sure the other person *heard* what

you said and *understood* what you meant.
4. Listen, listen, listen.
5. Respond nondefensively and without criticism.
6. Remember that the person you are talking to is more important than any issue you might be discussing.

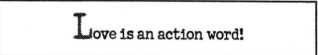

Love is an action word!

Make the Effort to Act Lovingly

Have you carefully considered the Bible's description of love in 1 Corinthians 13? It throbs with energetic words that demand action. According to God's own definition, love is:

- patient ... in all kinds of situations
- kind ... regardless of how others act
- confident ... trusts others because of self-confidence
- content ... not envious
- generous ... thoughtful of needs of others
- polite ... uses good manners
- not demanding ... considerate
- approachable ... easy to communicate with
- forgiving ... pardons misbehavior
- nonjudgmental ... not a faultfinder
- just ... seeks fairness
- loyal ... a friend at all times
- believing ... looks for the best

- hopeful … trusts for the best
- enduring … steadfast in perseverance

You can germinate the seeds of love within yourself. Open your eyes to the possibilities of action as you seek to love people for whom you otherwise never would have cared. As she passed through downtown, a friend of mine saw a homeless woman shivering in the cold. She said to God, "Why did you permit this? Why don't you do something about it?"

Later that day, still troubled by the image of the cold, helpless woman, she repeated her prayer, "God, why don't you do something about it?"

In her heart she heard the answer. God said: "But I did do something about it; I showed this homeless woman to you."

> **W**hen you DO loving things,
> loving feelings will be created.

Make the Effort to Pray

Prayer is a mighty and mysterious force in the life of a believer. It builds a bridge from our broken human world to the perfect and powerful kingdom of God. In fact, it brings us into that kingdom and places our lives under the protection and care of the King of the Universe.

Prayer does several things for our relationships. One of the key purposes of prayer is described in the book used with Alcoholics Anonymous:

If you have a resentment you want to be free of, if you will pray for the person or the thing that you resent, you will be free. If you will ask in prayer for everything you want for yourself to be given to them, you will be free. Ask for their health, their prosperity, their happiness, and you will be free. Even when you don't really want it for them, and your prayers are only words, go ahead and do it anyway. Do it every day for two weeks and you will find you have come to mean it and to want it for them, and you will realize that where you used to feel bitterness and resentment and hatred, you now feel compassion and understanding and love.[1]

Of course, prayer does far more than change our heart toward difficult people. Prayer releases God's supernatural power into the situation about which we are praying. No one really understands how or why God responds to prayer. But Jesus repeatedly told us to pray about everything, great and small. And he advised us to pray persistently.

In prayer, we acknowledge that we are incapable of dealing with things on our own. We can confront the behavior of others, but we cannot change it. We can reach out in love toward others, but we cannot put love in their hearts for us. We can attempt to communicate our best intentions, but we cannot direct the impact of our words or control the way those words are understood. Through prayer, we invite God into the circumstances, asking him to do the things we cannot do, to work in the silence, the solitude, the hidden places of the other person's life.

In addition, prayer makes it possible for us to genuinely "let go and let God." As we pray, we relinquish to him the burden of the bruised or broken relationship. We allow him to do his mighty, miraculous work in the heart of the other person.

Prayer also involves listening. As we pray, we seek the wisdom of God and sit quietly to hear his voice. Often, he will speak through his Word (if you don't have an up-to-date translation of the Bible, you might want to buy one). We all need to make conscious contact with God through prayer, and we need to do it every day. Ask for his will to be done in your earthly relationships, just as his will is done in heaven. Ask for the power of his Spirit to carry out what he desires in your life. Ask him to release supernatural love into your life, and into the life of your porcupine person.

As answers to prayer come, bringing direction and guidance from God, you may find yourself led to take new steps toward reconciliation. Prayer probably won't bring your efforts to an end. God may speak to you and ask more of you than you ever intended to give. God expects you to do your part. As the old aphorism says,

> Pray toward heaven
> but row toward shore!

Make the Effort to Walk in the Light

By now it should be clear that loving again really does take EFFORT on our part; loving feelings do not return simply because we want them to. (The old maxim "Time heals all wounds" is not always true. Sometimes "Time wounds all heels" is closer to the truth!) If our goal is to honestly reconcile with our porcupine person, then we must become physically, mentally and spiritually involved in the process. If we want a stronger, clearer vision and spiritual light, then we must love in action.

Anyone who claims to live in God's light, and hates a brother or sister is still in the dark. It's the person who loves a brother and sister who dwells in God's light and doesn't block the light from others. But whoever hates is still in the dark, stumbles around in the dark, doesn't know which end is up, blinded by the darkness.

1 JOHN 2:8 THE MESSAGE

Reflections

1. Think of an area in which better understanding might improve your relationship with your difficult person. Make the effort to dig for this information and acquire understanding (sensitively and carefully, please!). Write down the results.

2. List your most common emotional defenses, that is, the habits or patterns you use to protect yourself from being hurt. Make the decision to increase your openness by decreasing your defenses.

3. Is it difficult for you to communicate with your porcupine

person? Make a list of at least five ways you could improve conversations, and try them out.

4. What are some loving actions you could take to show your difficult person that you are making an effort toward a better relationship?

5. Make a list of blessings you'd like for yourself. Pray them every day for your difficult person, too.

6. Recall the good old days when love for this person came more easily to you. Picture places you've gone and laughter you've shared. Is it possible your viewpoint has changed more than he or she has changed?

TEN

F=Forgiveness Is Essential

I sat in the dentist's chair and listened compliantly to his usual lecture. "How often do you floss?" he asked as he poked and probed with something that strongly resembled an instrument of torture.

"Oh, I'll admit I forget to a lot...."

He stopped his poking and looked at me gravely. "When you choose not to take care of your teeth, you are choosing to accept misery. When you refuse to floss you are creating an environment in which all kinds of bad things can develop—decay, virus, inflammation, you name it. But you are a big girl now. The choice is up to you."

I was struggling to forgive someone at the time of my dental appointment. Maybe that's why the doctor's words about flossing seemed to apply to forgiveness. This is what I understood: whether we're concerned about our teeth or our hearts, when we refuse to remove things that are hidden in dark places, bad things grow. The sign on the dentist's wall made a lot of sense:

There is nothing the physician can do
which will overcome
what the patient will NOT do.

Like the other ABCs of learning to love again, forgiveness is an indispensable part of the reconciliation process. Refusing to take this step of faith eventually produces a condition that even the Great Physician cannot overcome. In some situations, it may be the most important element and the first effort that has to be made. Until we forgive our porcupine people for their misbehavior, we will always have a blockage in our ability to love them again. In our hearts, a root of bitterness can breed mistrust, hostility and a judgmental spirit. Any and all of these ugly viruses will cause problems we never dreamed of (if you think a dental root canal is bad, try an emotional one!). Better we get to work and clean up our heart's environment, letting in the Lord's cleansing light as we determine to develop and maintain a forgiving, loving spirit.

Grudges are like grenades;
we'd better release them
before they destroy us.

What Forgiveness Isn't

While we're exploring the importance of forgiveness, it is essential for us to understand its limitations. Counselors David and Janet Congo cite four important points that are worth considering when we seek to forgive. In essence, they explain what forgiveness is not

- *Forgiveness is not forgetting, ignoring, denying or pretending.* It is important to forgive the wrong done to us at its worst. This means no watering down, no excuses for the offending person. If we forgive only a diluted version of the offense, we do not completely forgive.

- *Forgiveness is not acquittal.* There is no place in forgiveness for denying that the offense occurred. That requires dishonesty. When we forgive, we pardon for something that really happened, essentially saying, "You are guilty of hurting me, but you are also forgiven."

- *Forgiveness is not reconciliation.* Reconciliation requires two or more people to work toward rebuilding a healthy relationship. It only takes one person to forgive; the person we forgive need not participate.

- *Forgiveness is not instantaneous.* When we forgive someone, we may find ourselves needing to go through the same process again and again. When the old, angry emotions begin to resurface in our hearts, we have to stop and begin again: "Lord, I want to forgive _____. Please help me release these intense and powerful feelings to you. You deal with _____. I don't want to feel this way any longer."[1]

Forgiveness Releases Us, Not Others

I learned the power of forgiveness at a young age. As I mentioned before, when I was a new, teenage Christian, I was raped. The pregnancy that followed forced my young life in a direction that would forever rob me of my youth and innocence. As far as I could see, I had more than my share to forgive. Fortunately, the Christians who surrounded me with love during those difficult years were wise enough to counsel me about God's requirements for forgiveness.

In prayer there is a connection between what God does and what you do, Jesus told his disciples. "You can't get forgiveness from God, for instance, without also forgiving others. If you refuse to do your part, you cut yourself off from God's part" (Mt 6:14-15 THE MESSAGE).

In actuality, the rapist victimized me the first time, but if I had not forgiven him, I would have continued to be victimized by my own bitterness. Instead, because I was able to learn some invaluable principles from God's Word and through Christian friends, I was able to follow my heavenly Father's example. He is quick to forgive. He loves unconditionally. He has promised never to leave us or forsake us. Most of all he, the caring Father, gave his precious son for us.

If God was willing to forgive us, how can we do less for one another? He has told us what he expects. The rest is up to us.

One author puts it this way: "So often we view forgiveness as being for the other person. We say, 'I will never forgive him,' as though we are holding him to some form of punishment to be endured until we release him. No, we are the ones enduring; we endure the ravages of bitterness closing up our hearts."[2]

> Bitterness is a cup of poison
> that we must refuse to drink.

Resisting the Blame Game

Most of us have a tendency to blame others for our problems and then to hold those problems against them. This can be particularly true in our relationships with our parents. Did your parents blow it, like mine did? I am so grateful for a heavenly Father who has come to help me re-parent myself!

God really is our father. Even though our parents decided to make love, it was God who decided to make life. Each of us was God's decision! We can breathe a sigh of relief once we realize that none of us was truly "unwanted" or "illegitimate." Life belongs to God—without our parents' written permission!

> **V**iew your birth parents simply as the biological instruments of your existence.

Is your porcupine person one of your parents? Maybe both of them have done things for which you need to forgive them. If you find yourself saying, "Lee, you don't understand. I can never forgive them!" ask yourself a couple of questions: *Will blaming my parents help to fulfill the commandment "Honor your father and your mother"* (Ex 20:12)? *How would I feel if my own children regarded me as I am choosing to regard my parents?*

Think about how Jesus viewed his mother, Mary, and his earthly father, Joseph. Although he clearly respected and honored them both, he did not see them as particularly instrumental in forming the person he was becoming. In one instance, speaking of Mary, he said, "Who is my mother and who are my brothers?" (Mt 12:48). And as for the role of a father in his life, he exhorted his followers, "Do not call anyone on earth your father; for One is your Father, he who is in heaven" (Mt 23:9).

Modern psychology places a great deal of weight on the influence of parents upon our lives. Perhaps if we had a better connection with the parenting—and re-parenting—skills of our heavenly Father, we wouldn't endow our earthly parents with so much power. Consequently, we would have a less critical attitude toward them.

Forgive, Even When It Seems Impossible

Whether the perpetrators are parents, friends or strangers, some of the wrongs we suffer are so terrible that it is difficult to imagine finding the ability to forgive them. Thomas was a godly, patient man who worked in a parachurch ministry. Overworked and underpaid, in his desperate need for assistance, he teamed up with Jason, who was more than willing to help. At first, Thomas didn't realize that Jason was addicted to drugs. And once he found out about the drug issue, he had become so dependent on Jason's help that he decided to pray and hope for the best rather than fire him.

Actually, drugs were only part of the problem. After befriending Jason and trying to encourage him to get help with his addiction, Thomas discovered a brutal truth. Jason had been having sex with Thomas' wife—and daughter, resulting in his daughter getting pregnant. Eventually, ashamed and disenchanted with the family troubles, Thomas' wife divorced him.

Thomas was at the hospital when his beautiful daughter gave birth to his first grandson. His heart ached as she took the grandson and went home to Jason, with whom she had rented an apartment. The daughter was hoping Jason would divorce his wife of twenty years and leave his older children to stay with her and their newborn.

Forgive? Forget? After working through anger, hatred and even death wishes against Jason, Thomas eventually realized that a root of bitterness was choking the life out of him. Hard as it was, he knew what God wanted him to do. He couldn't prescribe behavior for his wife, his daughter or his former friend. But this Christian man figured the old adage must be true: "God's *callings* are God's *enablings*." He knew God had called him to love.

Love would have to begin with forgiveness. But to his amazement, forgiveness brought Thomas, broken as he was, to a place where he learned to believe, again, in love. Eventually God blessed him with remarriage.

> The important thing about your lot in life is whether you use it for building or for parking.

I heard concentration camp survivor Corrie ten Boom tell that once when she was speaking to a large audience, she spied one of her death camp's vicious guards staring back at her. There he was, actually sitting in the audience! Her heart went cold. She froze.

After the meeting, the former guard approached her. Corrie was overcome with emotions. For years she had imagined that if she ever encountered any of the people who had participated in the murder of her father and sister, she would attack him violently, at least with words. Yet now the worst of them all stood before her—and he was pleading for forgiveness. In that instant, Corrie's hard heart melted. Right then, God gave her the grace she needed. She forgave the guard.

> Insomuch as anyone pushes you nearer to God, he or she is your friend.

Cultivate a Forgiving Spirit

A friend of mine wrote me a scathing letter about our pastor. "Haven't you heard? He is unfaithful to his wife, and he is cheating the church out of thousands of dollars!"

I was shocked. I took the accusations directly to the pastor, quite certain that there was no truth in them. His reaction spoke volumes. There was no defensiveness, no porcupine posturing. He confirmed that he had heard there was a slanderous rumor being passed around and was hurt by it. But as he reread the letter he quickly said, "I find myself wanting to forgive this woman; someone has fed her lies, and she has chosen to believe them."

"You want to forgive her? Just like that? How can you do that?" His reaction didn't compute. He was genuinely feeling wounded; yet he was astonishingly quick to forgive. He didn't even take time for a pity party!

Later, he filled me in on a secret. Apparently, after I left, he found that he was also puzzled about his quick ability to pardon his offender. He had spoken aloud to God, "Lord, why is it that I still feel some degree of love for this old friend who is spreading such a vicious rumor?"

Immediately God had spoken to his spirit, "You love her because I love her, and because she loves me. That's enough."

Let not mercy and truth forsake you:
Bind them around your neck.

PROVERBS 3:3

When you are faced with the necessity to forgive, put this string of pearls around your neck: mercy and truth upon mercy and truth. Truth means we don't allow denial or dishonesty to be part of our assessment of the wrongful circumstances we are dealing with. Mercy means we will act with compassion because God has been compassionate with our sins. Both will be needed to do a thorough job of pardoning.

Another precious pearl is humility—a significant requirement of God. He expects it of us and will continue to develop it within us, working through our most difficult circumstances. I tremble when I read how God actually let Moses spend forty years wandering around in circles, in the wilderness, "to humble you and test you; to know what was in your heart" (Dt 8:2). God is in no hurry, friends. We know God resists the proud and gives grace to the humble. Truth, mercy and humility are invaluable assets when we face the task of forgiveness. And forgiveness is an indispensable step in learning to love again.

> If you want something you've never had, you have to be willing to do something you've never done.

Dr. Verle Bell, an award-winning psychiatrist who is also a pastor, makes a valuable statement: "We may be equating forgiveness with things like trusting, excusing and forgetting. We know all too well that we can't immediately turn around and trust someone who has hurt us. God certainly doesn't ask us to excuse that person's behavior. And we know we can never forget what's happened to us. So we end up crying out, 'God, I just can't do what you want. It's impossible for me to forgive!'

"To back up this approach, people sometimes quote the scripture which says, 'forgetting what lies behind and reaching forward to what lies ahead' (Phil 3:13 NASB). Let's assume that this particular verse really means forgetting anything from the past which tries to keep us from pushing forward to whatever God has for us. That word 'forgetting' still does not mean 'never thinking about or never feeling.' What forgetting really means is 'neglecting, not dwelling upon, not going round and round about something which we cannot change.'"[3]

> Forgiveness is well worth the effort it takes to yank our wills to the painful point of obedience.
>
> KAREN BURTON MAINS

Forgiveness and Acceptance

Have you ever encountered someone who is emotionally crippled? Some of the people in our lives may be genuinely incapable of behaving in a loving, nurturing or even fully acceptable way. Perhaps severe personality disorders handicap them. Or they may be involved in a sinful lifestyle that causes them to be completely self-absorbed. Sometimes these circumstances are temporary, and changes eventually occur. But often, especially with older adults, we are forced to come to terms with people who are simply not going to change, and their present state is nearly intolerable. When this happens, forgiveness does not involve the repentance of the other person. It is simply our choice to rid ourselves of bitter, angry feelings and to make some sort of amicable relationship possible.

My friend Gary had been wronged by his father over and over again. Even in adulthood, his dad's rejection of him (and Gary's children) hurt. After the latest blow, his dad firing him from the family business, Gary knew he was at a crossroads. Confrontation hadn't improved the situation. Avoiding the old man hadn't worked either. Finally, after much prayer, Gary became convinced that there was only one thing left to do. He decided to love his father. Gary made this decision; a new understanding dawned on him that he explained to me in this way: "I now recognize that my father is an emotional cripple. He simply does not own the capacity for loving and caring. Regardless of what has made him this way, I must love him as he is. My desire would be to run an emotional marathon with my dad; but he can't even walk. So if the only run I can have with my dad is to (emotionally) push him around the mall in a wheelchair, I choose to do that."

> **A**bove all these things put on love.
> COLOSSIANS 3:14

P.B. (Bunny) Wilson's excellent book, *Betrayal's Baby,* addresses the removal of bitterness from our lives. In it she provides a list of steps for individuals who are learning to forgive. With her permission, I have adapted it slightly.

1. Give up your right to judge why others have done what they've done. Forgive them in your heart.
2. Confess your fault in harboring resentment and hurt.
3. When you contact the offending person, make sure that your only goal is reconciliation.
4. Be committed to loving this person unconditionally. You won't be as likely to be hurt if you are not expecting anything in return, and that includes a kind word.
5. When you are not looking for a particular response, you can't be disappointed and it will allow the Holy Spirit time to bring about reconciliation in the relationship.
6. Always have a spirit of gratitude as you observe the slightest bit of thawing in the relationship. Remember, we all see through a "mirror dimly" (1 Cor 13:12), and things may be better than you think.
7. Remember that the reason you've been hurt so deeply is because of the depth of your love for the other person. Don't let another day pass without taking steps toward reconciliation.[4]

My friend Jennifer has a difficult time talking. Her ability to speak was lost, along with many other bodily functions, at age twenty-one when a drug-addicted illegal immigrant drove head-on into her car. Life, as she had known it, was lost. Her future was shattered. Her body was irreparably broken. Her hopes for the future, like the car she was driving, were twisted beyond recognition. It was easy to be enraged, natural to be embittered.

Nonetheless, Jennifer made a conscious decision to forgive. She released herself and her life to the One who made her in the first place. She exchanged self-pity for peace, bitterness for a beautiful spirit. Even more amazing, Jennifer absolutely exudes gratitude. Words don't come easily through her lips anymore. Yet, from her wheelchair, she painstakingly affirms, "But the Lord has blessed me so much! God is so good to me!"

> Happiness does not depend on what's happening, but on what you DO about what's happening!

Reflections

1. List any grudges you may be holding against your difficult person. Pray that God will help as you begin the forgiveness process.
2. Are you holding anything against your parents? Take steps

to release them from your anger and resentment. If necessary, ask them to forgive you for any behavior that resulted from your lack of forgiveness.

3. What is the most unforgivable situation you have ever faced? Have you resolved it, with God's help? If not, begin today.

4. Reflect upon truth, mercy and humility. How do they fit into forgiveness?

5. Could you possibly be dealing with an emotional cripple? Write your thoughts about this possibility. (Don't expect or require a cripple to run beside you.)

ELEVEN

G=God Is on the Side of Love

My friend Lisa sat at my dining room table, sipping tea and shaking her head. "I just don't get what happened, Lee," she told me. "I used to feel close to God. I used to have a genuine love relationship with him. Somehow it drained away over the years. If I were honest, I'd have to say God let me down too many times in my hour of need. Sure, I believe he has all the power, but he doesn't seem to bother to intervene for me. Then there was the church split. After all those years of service, I was devastated. It's not fair."

Of course, Lisa is right. Life is not fair. And yet, hard as it is to add up, our sovereign God, who rules over every aspect of our lives, is a fair and just God. If you have a hard time grasping that idea, join the club. But experience will eventually prove to you that he is in control, his timing is perfect and he doesn't make mistakes.

What is your view of God? How do you see him? As a divine butler who will bring your every request? As "God is rad, he's my Dad!"—a permissive parent who never disciplines his kids? As the sadistic designer of natural disasters or as an old, grumpy, hard-to-please judge?

None of those descriptions of the creator of the universe comes remotely close to the reality of our God. Knowing him and making him known are among the responsibilities we share as believers. Do you know God? Do you trust him?

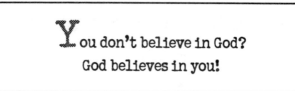

You don't believe in God?
God believes in you!

The Bible's picture of God is clear. He is the deity full of love for his creation, one who "so loved the world that He gave His only begotten Son" (Jn 3:16). God's ultimate sacrifice on our behalf is Christ dying in our place so we could live. The apostle John explains it simply: "He who has the Son has life" (1 Jn 5:12). Not only did God restore life to his crucified son; he wants to breathe new life into us—into our heartaches, disappointments, broken relationships and the injustices that led to them. How desperately we all need to restore our love for him, so he will be fully free to restore our lives to us and enable us to love porcupine people.

Just giving a nod to God or joining in on an occasional religious meeting isn't the answer. We have to actually plant the seeds of faith in Jesus Christ into our own hearts. Our faith doesn't have to be as big as our problems; even a mustard seed–size will do the trick! As you read further, I hope a new picture of the true God will emerge in your spirit. It will be a portrait of the God of love, the one who cared enough to send the very best.

I pray that you, being rooted and established in LOVE, may have power...to grasp how wide and long and high and deep is the love of Christ.

EPHESIANS 3:17-19 NIV

Hothouse Living?

When I was a teenager, I received Christ at a Billy Graham crusade in Philadelphia. To be honest with you, I misunderstood what Dr. Graham meant in talking about a new life. I thought this new life would be relatively free of problems once I got the right connection with God. I couldn't wait to have my crummy problems (magically!) squared away and get the fresh start Billy talked about. I imagined God putting his children in a little hothouse that was climate-controlled and sheltered from life's storms. My life changed for the better in some ways. But before long it became more difficult than ever. I had a lot to learn.

God was with me in the worst of times—rape, pregnancy, adoption and the emotional aftermath. But he hadn't prevented any of those difficult circumstances from happening. This was something like my friend who received Christ in a church service. He felt brand new on the inside, absolutely bursting with joy. But as he bounded out to his car in the parking lot, he found the car had two flat tires. Before he realized what he was saying, he blurted out, "C'mon, God. This isn't what I signed up for in your meeting!"

> **R**edemption is not an exemption
> from life's problems!

We'd better realize that the "contract" we signed with God is blank; he will fill in the terms one day at a time. Our security doesn't lie in promises of earthly perfection. It lies in the fact that heaven's King is resident within us, empowering us to face the worst of times and go on loving him and others, as well as blessing us—when he sees fit—with the best of times.

Unfortunately, some Christians have lost that loving feeling toward God because, from their perspective, he didn't come through for them in a time of need, performing for them when they wanted his help the most. A common misunderstanding about God is that he is a kind of celestial slot machine: if we put in enough prayers, he'll shoot out a jackpot answer. Nor does God manage a divine pizza service that delivers all our triple-decker, deluxe requests in half an hour or less. God's Word tells us a great deal about his character, but we don't always want to hear what he has to say.

"My dear child, don't shrug off God's discipline, but don't be crushed by it either. It's the child he loves that he disciplines; the child he embraces, he also corrects.... Only irresponsible parents leave children to fend for themselves. Would you prefer an irresponsible God?"

HEBREWS 12:11 THE MESSAGE

God is a wise parent who knows the end from the beginning, an eternal being who is interested in our ultimate good both in this life and the life to come. He invariably acts with our best interests in mind. But because we are locked in time, we are concerned primarily with our immediate good. We are not given the assurance that we'll immediately *see* ultimate good in our struggles and challenges on this earth. We do have the assurance that he does work all things for good. Our job is to trust in the ultimate positive outcome of our immediate troubles. That means exercising faith. It also means keeping our relationship with him free of spiritual sulks.

When your situation didn't work out in your favor, did you lose faith? Has disappointment over some unanswered prayer caused a blockage in your prayer life? Does a simmering, unexpressed resentment toward God keep you from surrendering your will to his? These obstacles can be overcome when you correct your viewpoint of God, acknowledging the reality of his loving, but sometimes mysterious, character.

Steps Back Into Faith

As we seek reconciliation with God, we can walk through the steps to loving a porcupine person, and apply these steps toward him.

A = Accept the fact that God loves you so much he was willing to send Jesus to die for your sins.

B = Believe God has reached out to you by sending Christ and that he wants the best for you.

C = Confront your feeling of disappointment in God or his church or both.

D = Decide that your relationship with God is more important than any other situation or circumstance.

E = Expend effort to begin a new, humble walk with him. Get out that Bible again!

F = Forgive God (even though he is incapable of doing wrong). Equally necessary is forgiving yourself.

Return to Your First Love

In the last book of the Bible, God speaks to a group of Christians against whom he has one complaint. He says, "You have forsaken your first love" (Rv 2:4 NIV). By this the Lord means that these otherwise faithful believers have gradually let their initial excitement and enthusiasm for him and his gospel slip away. If this describes you (at one time or another, it describes all of us), here are three suggestions:

1. REMEMBER those times of your first love, when your whole heart was turned toward heaven and your thoughts and emotions were full to overflowing with love for Jesus. What were the circumstances surrounding your initial decision to follow the Lord? Try to recall your reaction to the words you heard at that time. Were you moved emotionally? Were you stimulated intellectually? If someone who shared that event with you is still in your life, take the time to talk to him or her. Try to recreate in your heart the day you "fell in love" with the Lord.

2. REPENT and turn back to those early days. Is anything standing between you and the Lord right now? Are you involved in a habit, addiction or sin that feels like a wedge between you and him? Are you angry with him? Have you begun to doubt his love?

It's important to know that he wants you to come just the way you are. You don't have to get all cleaned up; he already knows how you look and feel with all your sins, doubts, hurts, guilt and fears. He is waiting for you right now. Like the father of the New Testament's Prodigal Son, your heavenly Father is watching for you to come down the road, awaiting your arrival with open arms.

3. REPEAT the behavior you exhibited when you first met the Lord, even if you don't feel like it right now. Love is a principle, not an emotion. You've heard that before, haven't you? I keep repeating it because it is both true and essential to the successful Christian life. Just as loving others is a principle, so is loving God. You don't have to work yourself into an emotional state of mind to approach him. Just speak his name. If you don't know what else to say, pray that timeless prayer, "Jesus, Son of God, Savior, have mercy on me." He will!

Fanatics or the "Frozen Chosen"?

Perhaps you are wondering if your Christian experience is supposed to be emotional. As I travel and speak in all kinds of church settings across the United States, I've found God moving in many different settings. I've come to this conclusion:

God loves diversity! From what I've witnessed, God is not restricted to keeping company with clergy who wear robes, nor is his sovereignty lessened by emotionally expressed worship.

Whatever the emotional style of the service I attend, rather than sit with a judgmental spirit, I try to stir up my unashamed first love for the Lord. As his bride, I don't think it would please Christ, the Bridegroom, if I responded to his proposal by saying, "Sure, I'd like to marry you, but I don't want any of that emotional stuff. I'll work for you, yes, but don't expect me to put my arms around you and tell you how wonderful you are. I'll take care of the money and keep things running smoothly, but don't try getting intimate with me."

Surely this is not what Jesus wants in his spouse. He wants a bride who loves him passionately, with heart, soul, mind and strength. So when I'm faced with a "wild and crazy" display of affection for God in church, I'm reminded that he often chooses the foolish and unsophisticated things of this world to confound the wise.

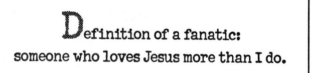

Definition of a fanatic:
someone who loves Jesus more than I do.

Disasters: Acts of God?

In spite of the Father's immeasurable love for us, all too often some injured person will look skyward and sarcastically say, "Thanks, God! Thanks a lot! Like I really needed that...."

While God is keenly aware of the injustices in life, the Lord also recognizes the human right to free will (although sometimes I think God would like to do a free-will recall!). Because God was not into creating clones or robots, he made human beings capable of voluntarily choosing whether to trust him, thank him and serve him—no matter what. Today, many suffer man's inhumanity to man, because man's free will also allows him (or her!) to be cruel, hateful and deadly. When one person makes a wrong choice, others inevitably suffer.

I'm convinced God is the source of love, not the source of the evil that happens in our world. Have you seen the bumper sticker that says something akin to "Fecal Matter Happens"? It's true. But it is rarely an accident. So much of life's worst messes are the result of people's sins, known and unknown, seen and unseen. Moreover, the kingdoms of this world are apparently, at least somewhat, under Satan's jurisdiction. During Jesus' time of temptation, when Satan offered to give him all the kingdoms of this world, Jesus did not argue with his adversary, claiming that the world was not Satan's to dole out. Let us keep in mind that we do have a ruling enemy, and that the world's darkness belongs to him, not to God. Maybe someone ought to pass this on to the insurance industry, which typically won't pay for earthquake damage, calling it an "act of God." But the prophet Elijah experienced "the Lord was not in the earthquake," but in a "still small voice" (1 Kgs 19:11).

Earthquakes are not an act of Father God; they are an act of Mother Nature!

Who's to Blame?

My friend, an incest victim, asked me, "Where was God for me when I was being raped by my father?" I know God didn't cause it, but God sure could have prevented it!

"God was aware. It didn't escape him," I answered. "Where was he? He was right there, weeping along with you."

The theory "God should have stopped that" is part of the fairy-tale kind of thinking I refer to as *the Cinderella syndrome.* God is not a fairy godfather in the sky who continuously intervenes in the affairs of life, waving a magic wand. He won't suddenly make it all right with a big "bibbity-bobbity-boo." But ...

> While God may not interfere with life's tragedies, he will redeem their consequences!

Discovering My Own Ultimate Good

My own life experience dramatically confirms God's redemption of tragic circumstances. The "whys" I struggled with regarding my rape and pregnancy were answered a few years ago in one spectacular, life-changing phone call. That call convinced me that God's ways are, indeed, far above our ways. An unfamiliar woman's voice announced to me that she was my daughter, the baby I had given up for adoption at birth more than twenty years before! Can you imagine how the tears flowed during that shocking conversation? Julie's growing-up

PROPERTY OF
HIGH POINT PUBLIC LIBRARY
HIGH POINT, NORTH CAROLINA

experience had been fine. Her parents were good people. But, like many adoptees, she sensed a "missing piece" in her own life. My subsequent reunion with Julie resulted in the writing of *The Missing Piece*, to encourage others who had faced similarly unexplainable events.[1] I am fully convinced that God is always working behind the scenes for those who love him.

In the middle of life's most heart-wrenching situation, please keep in mind baseball legend Yogi Berra's not-so-silly quip: "It ain't over 'til it's over." We don't know the truth about our circumstances until we hear from the Truth himself, Jesus Christ.

> **When you cannot trace God's hands, you can still trust God's love.**

The Breaking of a Dream

Just like a child would bring a toy
To Daddy's lap to mend,
I took my broken dream to God;
I knew he was my friend.
But then I wouldn't leave the toy
In his hands to do the work,
No, I kept reaching out for it,
And I'd accuse, "You shirk."
Finally, I grabbed it back,
"How could you be so slow?"
"Oh love," he said, "what can I do?"
"You never did let go."

Our Source of Love

In order to restore that loving feeling to our relationships, we'll have to be attached to the source of love. The Bible describes God's essence as "love" (1 Jn 4:8), though not all of God's children reflect that. Too many of us have had discouraging and disillusioning experiences among Christians friends or in church and have turned our back on organized religion. Many of us, whether we admit it or not, have come to agree with that weary cliché: "There are too many hypocrites in the church!"

I would like to apologize to those of you who have been wounded by someone in the church. Would you accept my apology, on behalf of God's people? We have messed up, it's true. There are many hypocrites within the Body of Christ and many abusive Christians. Within the stained-glass walls, I have experienced my share of betrayal and hardheartedness, too.

But then, so did Jesus. Talk about mistreatment at the hands of religion! Most of the problems and opposition Christ encountered were from the religious community of his day. Those "spiritual" leaders stretched and strained Scripture verses in order to use them against him. They falsely accused him. They rejected him. Had I been God, I would have been tempted to zap them from heaven. A little hail, perhaps? Maybe throw in a plague of frogs!

The religious leaders stirred up the crowd against Jesus, screaming for his crucifixion and the release of Barabbas. Jesus found himself alone, asking God, "Why have you forsaken me?" (Mt 27:46). All the while, God was there, perhaps regretting having to watch the agony of his Son, who had volunteered to be the sacrificial lamb for all humankind. Christ's death secured for us a place in God's family, adopted by a father declaring, "I know the plans I have for you ... plans to prosper you and not to harm you, plans to give you a hope and a future" (Jer 29:11 NIV).

> The hands that reach out to us from God don't reach to wound us; but they are wounded, nail-scarred hands.

I asked one contented Christian friend (an endangered species, by the way), "Have you ever been disillusioned with God because of people in the church?"

My friend smiled and shook her head, "No, but maybe that's because I never had illusions about how *perfect* the church should be. I'm learning to accept all people as imperfect and struggling. Jesus is the only one I can fully rely on. There is only one prince who has said 'I will never leave you nor forsake you' (Heb 13:5), and that's the Prince of Peace!"

Reflections

1. Has God disappointed you? Did you assume he would automatically protect you from evil? Write a letter to him about what happened.

2. If you are still angry with God, why not confess that now? This could remove a huge obstacle to your loving him again. Add to your letter your willingness to let go of your resentment toward him. Ask him to forgive you for not trusting him with the situation.

3. Is it possible God has been wrongly accused of causing some disaster in your life? Accept the fact that, while God does not cause the evil, he is the only one who can turn evil into good in your life. Thank him for what he is doing—right now—to work all things together for good in your life.

TWELVE

H=His Love Never Fails!

The more often we walk alongside, follow and obey Jesus, holding his nail-scarred hand, the clearer the picture becomes of who we are and, as a result, how positively we can view even the most difficult people in our lives. It is possible that we have a problem loving a porcupine person because we don't love ourselves—a necessary step. (I don't mean an unhealthy overemphasis on self that leads to narcissism and stems from a big ego.) There is a kind of healthy self-love that allows us to live and let live, to appreciate the soul of another person instead of comparing and always hoping we'll win the who-is-the-greatest contest!

In our culture, an overemphasis on self-esteem in schools is producing *over*confident *under*achievers. The emphasis on human acceptance is offered as society's cure-all. In this New Age mentality, we're told our greatest sin is not living up to our potential. In this climate, sports stars become heroes and icons, taunting, "I'm the greatest." Parallel this with the apostle Paul, who declared, "I'm the least," even though he had more than enough to boast about. Paul was highly educated, incomparably spiritual and a respected leader. Yet he declared all of that meant nothing to him; he counted it as dung (modern interpretation: *crap*). And look at the lives of Peter and John, unschooled, ordinary men. But the difference in their lives was recorded in Scripture: "others perceived ... that they had been with Jesus" (Acts 4:13 KJV).

There is a balance here. We want to love others, but first we must remember that charity begins with us. Remind yourself of these powerful truths:

- All my sins are forgiven through the cross (Eph 1:7).
- I am complete and whole in Christ (Col 2:10).
- My life is hidden with Christ in God (Col 3:3).
- I am acceptable to God in the Beloved (Christ) (Eph 1:6).
- The Spirit of God now lives inside me (1 Cor 6:19).
- In Christ, I am entirely set free (Jn 8:31-33).

The Spirit of Love

Love that wilt not let me go,
I rest my weary soul in thee;
I give thee back the life I owe,
That in thine ocean depths its flow
May richer, fuller be.

GEORGE MATHESON AND
ALBERT L. PEACE, 1882

God's Spirit surrounds us and permeates us with love. Oh, how we desire that the flow of God in us and through us be richer and fuller. Our desire will surely be met. For although love is not a spiritual gift bestowed upon us, there is a spirit of love which God has granted us.

For God has ... given us ... a spirit of power and of love.
2 TIMOTHY 1:7

God only asks that we be a people who resist evil and cling to that which is good. One of those good things is the choice we are making to love again. We are determined to see things in a new light now, the light of love. Seeing with clear eyes was a key theme in Jesus' teaching. We need to wash the darkness out of our eyes. The last thing God wants is that we remain hidden in the shadows of resentment and anger. He has called us OUT of darkness, into his marvelous light. The light of love will heal our eyes so we see more clearly. It will open our ears, so we can hear more sensitively. It will help us control our mouth, so our speech will be seasoned with salt.

Why do you look at the speck in your brother's eye, but do not notice the log that is in your own eye?
MATTHEW 7:3-5 NASB

As I've been practicing my own homemade brand of ophthalmology, I've been removing logs from my own eyes on a regular basis. Now I'm seeing more clearly, too. The specks that bugged me in my husband's eye don't look like such a big deal anymore. The career-mindedness of my stepdaughters doesn't seem as abrasive. The critical and overbearing personalities of my challenging people are not so pointed. I'm glimpsing God's purpose and experiencing his assistance as I learn to love my porcupine people.

When we are walking in love, we more clearly see God in our own lives and, working all around us, in the lives of others. The excellent book and Bible study *Experiencing God* by Henry Blackaby and Claude King encourages us to remember that God is working everywhere, and he wants to involve us in what he is doing.[1] This was the secret of Jesus' success. He said, "The son only does what he sees the Father doing ..." (Jn 5:19 LB). Christ's vision was so clear, so clean, so unobstructed by an unloving attitude that he could perfectly see and hear God. How I long for that! And Jesus said, "As the Father has sent me, I also send you" (Jn 20:21).

Four Essential Questions

As you seek to experience God's love in a more powerful way, it is important that you ask yourself key questions.

First of all, *can you see God at work in your circumstances right now?* If so, walk in his light, and refuse to allow your sight to be obscured by bad feelings toward other people. It may be true that in your church there are some shallow people, and even some flaky ones. But it is also true that many of his friends are there and that God may have brought you to that place much as he brought Esther into the king's palace to fulfill his purpose "for such a time as this" (Est 4:14).

Question number two: *Can you see God in your everyday*

activities? When you begin to practice walking in the light of love, you will notice that God is speaking to you through a book you are reading, through a movie you've seen, through your efforts in the garden. God will communicate with you; he only asks that you listen. And when your goal is loving others more effectively, you can be sure that he will help you, guide you and enable you in every aspect of the process.

Question number three: *Can you see God's purpose in exhorting you to love your porcupine person?* That could be a challenge, particularly if you are continually confronted with that person's difficult behavior or unkindness to you. However, the Lord may be planning to use this person to draw you closer to himself. Reconciliation is God's specialty. His desire is to reconcile the whole world to himself, and that is why he urges you and me to love one another.

If you love those who love you, what reward have you?

MATTHEW 5:46

Now consider question number four: *Who is the most difficult person in your life and why is he or she there?* Just to be offensive and abrasive? Is your porcupine person there simply to irritate and worry you?

As always, Jesus was right in reminding us, "If a son ... asks for a fish, will he give him a serpent? Or if he asks for an egg, will you give him a scorpion?" (Lk 11:11). If we have asked God for bread and think he has given us a stone, maybe we had better take another look. As we change our point of view, I believe many scorpionlike people will be reinterpreted as gifts. Perhaps they are nutritional fish after all, food to grow on. Maybe some of the stonelike individuals in our lives can become more palatable.

With God All Things Are Possible

Close your eyes and get a better vision of your porcupine person. See this person as he or she is. Then endeavor to picture him or her acting affectionately toward you. Pray for that person to realize God's plan for his or her life. See this person changed by the power of the love of God. Then open your eyes and begin walking and believing this is possible.

In Hannah Hurnard's classic allegory, *Hinds Feet on High Places*, the main character, Much Afraid, was learning the lessons of love as the shepherd planted the seed of love in her heart. Finally she developed hinds' feet so she could leap upon the mountains with the shepherd, who asked her what lessons of love she had learned. Much Afraid replied, "I learned everything that happens in life ... can be changed if I treat it with love, forgiveness and obedience to your will. You let us meet with the bad and wrong things to be made into something beautiful. You want us to overcome evil with good."[2]

In light of my understanding of God's plan for spiritual transformation, I can envision the lineup outside the pearly gates. The crowd is backed up; there is heavy traffic this eternal day. And as I wait in line, I wonder what criteria will determine the separation at the head of the line, sent to the left or to the right. St. Peter stands at the head of the line, pointing his finger in one direction or the other. What is God's litmus test? I wonder if they are handing out questionnaires. Do I have to answer some riddle correctly in order to be admitted into eternal life? Are the questions multiple choice, something like this?

What denomination are you?
A. Baptist
B. Orthodox
C. Pentecostal
D. Other _____

How were you baptized?
A. Sprinkled
B. Immersed
C. In the name of Jesus (only)

How do you stand on the Millenium?
A. Pre-trib
B. Post-trib
C. Pan-trib (It'll all pan out in the end)

I start chewing my nails again. I have received Jesus—that base is covered—but is there something more required? Have I enough Bible knowledge to pass? I am getting closer to the interrogation area and my palms are sweaty. I hear someone say, "Lee, next." To my surprise the examiner does not hand me a questionnaire but reaches out with a sort of heavenly stethoscope, placing it against my heart.

St. Peter asks, "Do you hear the beating of life?"

"Yes," replies the examiner.

"Where there is life, there is love. Enter in."

I am thrilled. No other test? No qualifying checklist? Just a simple check for the heartbeat of Christ within? "He who has the Son has life," says 1 John 5:12.

Yes, it's that simple. If you have chosen to receive Christ's death as a sacrifice for your sin, and if you have invited him to be resident in your life, you have life. And that life will empower you to love porcupine people, yourself and every person who crosses your path.

Now, seek to communicate that love.

And this I pray, that your love may abound still more and more.

PHILIPPIANS 1:9-10

NOTES

ONE
The Fruit of Love

1.Adapted from Tim Hansel, *You Gotta Keep Dancin'* (Colorado Springs, Colo.: Victor, 1985), 57.

THREE
Enemies: You Gotta Love 'Em!

1.Richard McBrient, "Catholicism," *Christianity Today,* January 8, 1996, 53.
2.Joseph Stowell, *Loving Those We'd Rather Hate* (Chicago: Moody, 1994), 15.
3.Julie Duin, "Norma McCorvey: The Conversion of 'Jane Roe,'" *Charisma Magazine,* July 9, 1996, 61.

FOUR
Relationships: The Ties That Bind (and Gag)

1.Lyric excerpts of "Do You Love Me?" by Sheldon Harnick and Jerry Bock, © 1964 (renewed 1992) by Mayerling Productions, Ltd. Administered by R&H Music and Jerry Bock Enterprises (USA). Reprinted by permission. All rights reserved.

FIVE
A = Accept Them ... Just As They Are

1.Rich Buhler, *Love, No Strings Attached* (Nashville: Thomas Nelson, 1987), 29.

SIX
B = Believe the Best!

1.Dr. James Dobson, "Reliving Twenty-five Years Together," *Focus on the Family* magazine, August 1985, 4.
2.Charles Spurgeon, as quoted in the *Joyful Noiseletter, Fellowship of Merry Christians,* March 1993, 2.

SEVEN
C = Confront With Care

1.Dr. Gary Roseberg, *Dr. Roseberg's Do-It-Yourself Relationship Mender* (Colorado Springs, Colo.: Focus on the Family, 1992).
2.David Augsburger, *Caring Enough to Confront* (Ventura, Calif.: Regal, 1981).
3.John Nieder and Thomas Thompson, *Forgive and Love Again* (Eugene, Ore.: Harvest House, 1991), 57.

EIGHT
D = Decide to Improve Your Relationship

1.Hannah Hurnard, *Mountains of Spices* (London: Olive Press, 1959), 55.

NINE
E = Effort Means Hard Work

1.W. Claire, *God, Help Me Stop!* (San Diego, Calif.: Books West, 1982), 126.

TEN
F = Forgiveness Is Essential

1.David and Janet Congo, *The Power of Love* (Chicago: Moody, 1993), 26.
2.Joseph Biuso, M.D., and Brian Newman, D.Phil., *Receiving Love* (Colorado Springs, Colo.: Victor, 1996), 74.
3.Dr. Verle Bell, *True Freedom* (Ann Arbor, Mich.: Servant, 1993), 68.
4.P.B. Wilson, *Betrayal's Baby* (Dexter, N.Y.: New Dawn, 1992), 38.

ELEVEN
G = God Is on the Side of Love

1.Lee Ezell, *The Missing Piece* (Ann Arbor, Mich.: Servant, 1992).

TWELVE
H = His Love Never Fails!

1.Henry Blackaby and Claude King, *Experiencing God* (Nashville, Tenn.: Broadman & Holman, 1993), 46.
2.Hannah Hurnard, *Hinds Feet on High Places* (Shippensburg, Penn.: Destiny Image, 1993), 107.

241.4 E99P c.1
Ezell, Lee.
Porcupine people : learning
to love the unlovable /

PROPERTY OF
HIGH POINT PUBLIC LIBRARY
HIGH POINT, NORTH CAROLINA